Sing for Joy

Songs and Activities for Elementary Children

C0-EFM-119

We extend our grateful appreciation to the members of the development team:
Gary Alan Smith, *Music Editor*
Nylea L. Butler-Moore, *Project Editor*
Timothy Edmonds
Pamela Ramp Schneller
Claudia Smith
Deb Smith

Abingdon Press
Nashville

SING FOR JOY

ISBN 0-687-20597-2

93 94 95 96 97 98 99 00 01 02—10 9 8 7 6 5 4 3 2 1

MANUFACTURED IN THE UNITED STATES OF AMERICA

Contents

 Suitable for the youngest children in the age group.

Helping Children Explore the World of Music

Nylea L. Butler-Moore

In the song, "God's World Is Filled with Music," author Camille Kennedy expresses her belief that melody is all around us, in the singing of the birds, in the sounds of rain and wind, and in the prayerful songs of little children. Stanza 3 claims, "Could we but stop and listen, there's melody ev'rywhere." "Stop and listen"—these are key words for those of us who teach music to children. To hear, to *really* hear the music of creation, and melodies and rhythms as traditionally defined, we must first stop and listen. Once we have heard and learned the melodies, we can help children stop, listen, and explore the world of music.

Enthusiasm Is Contagious

If you are enthusiastic about music and are thoroughly prepared to teach, the children will most likely be eager to learn. As frightening and miraculous as it seems, children will take their cues from you and will imitate your attitudes, skills, and level of enthusiasm.

As a teacher who has planned and prepared, you will communicate importance to what is being taught and will help avert potential discipline problems. Since most discipline problems occur as children "tune-out" rather than "tune-in," one of our most important goals is to *engage* the children in music making so that they learn almost without realizing it. The children then begin to think of music as a natural expression of who they are.

Preparing to Teach

As you prepare to teach, remember that music is one of a child's natural, creative responses to God's world. Music helps children:

- Express thoughts and feelings about God, self, and others
- Experience God's grace and grow spiritually
- Define their world
- Embrace their cultural traditions
- Become aware of the beliefs and ideas of others
- Develop essential motor, verbal, social, reading, mathematical, and memory skills
- Have increased self-esteem and a sense of self-worth

Get to know your children—their personalities, musical skills, ability to interact in group situations, and willingness to try new things. Make a special effort to know their voices individually and in a group. Plan music activities that will meet the needs of the children and will reach the specific goals you have in mind. Remember that intentional, thoughtful planning is a key to successful musical experiences.

Planning Tips

Plan as far in advance as possible, and get special events on the church or school calendar quickly. Coordinate your plans with all other persons involved—the accompanist, music helpers, minister of music, pastor, and so forth. Also inform the children's parents of your plans and intentions, and encourage them to participate in music making with their children.

Remember that your teaching situation is unique, and what works for another teacher may not work for you. Write your goals and plans on paper. Use the plans as guides, changing them, if necessary, to fit the current needs of the children.

Seek new and better ways of teaching. Adapt ideas and resources to your individual situation. Explore new ideas by reading, attending workshops, planning with team members and helpers, talking to other teachers of music, and trying new ideas with the children.

Selecting Music

Review a song thoroughly before including it in your teaching plans. Ask yourself the following questions.

- What truths (or untruths) does the song present?
- What words or concepts may be difficult for the children to grasp?
- What are the potential melodic and rhythmic problem spots?
- What is the mood of the song?
- Is the song vocally, textually, and musically appropriate for the group of children that will sing it?
- What teaching method would best introduce the song?
- For what occasion will the song be taught, and what are my teaching goals regarding the song?
- Does the song encourage the singers to expand their musical, spiritual, and cultural "horizons"?

Choose texts and music that are appropriate for the age level. If a text you wish to teach contains abstract or symbolic language that children would have trouble understanding, either choose another song or plan to explain the problematic text. Children should always understand the basic meaning of the texts they sing. Quiz them often by asking simple questions about the words. (Consider the song, "Come! Come! Everybody Worship," on page 64. Ask the children who is being worshiped and who should join us in worship. Ask them why we should "worship and remember to keep the Sabbath day," and so forth.)

The vocal range, the rhythmic difficulty, and the interval structure of a song should also be age-level appropriate. We should want children not merely to sing, but to sing well, "in their prettiest voices." In order for them to do so, we should avoid songs with ranges too low or too high. Having children consistently sing songs in inappropriate ranges can damage their voices. We should encourage them to sing in their true ranges, while gently helping them to expand the scope of their voices. (See **"Warm-ups and Vocal Production"** for more discussion on this topic.)

Basic Ranges

(from *Directing the Children's Choir* by Shirley W. McRae, pages 41, 43, 44, 46)

Learning the Music

Know the music, by memory if at all possible, before you attempt to teach it to the children. Write out the text to help you learn it. By isolating the words from the music, you can more easily focus on the content and structure of the text. Rhyming words, repeated phrases, and metrical form quickly become apparent. These elements can be pointed out to the children as you teach them the song.

Paraphrase the text and summarize its meaning in your own words. If you don't understand the text, how can the children?

Read the text aloud with expression, phrasing, and inflection. Reflect the mood of the text in the way you read the words, breathing in the appropriate places as if you were singing the song. Then, speak the text in the notated rhythm, using the same expression as before.

An easy way to begin learning the melody is to learn the melodic rhythm first. If you have spoken the text in rhythm, then you already know the rhythm of the melody.

Sing the melody on a neutral syllable such as "mah" or "loo," or on sol-fa syllables (do, re, mi, fa, sol, la, ti) until you can sing it smoothly and without mistakes. You could also sing the melody using rhythm words

(for example, "ta" for a quarter note, "tee-tee" for two eighth notes, "toe" for a half note, and so on). Finally, combine the melody and the words.

These same techniques of learning new music, along with many others, can be used in teaching songs to the children.

Ways to Teach a Song

It would be almost impossible to count the many ways of teaching a song. There are probably as many ways of teaching as there are teachers—maybe more!

Consider activities that incorporate visual, physical, and aural experiences. Alternate between periods of concentration and relaxation in the music lessons, and make the transitions from one song (or activity) to another as smooth as possible. Remembering that music experiences should be child-centered, strive to make lessons fun and enjoyable. David Bone, a church musician who works with both children and adults, suggests structuring your lesson in this way.

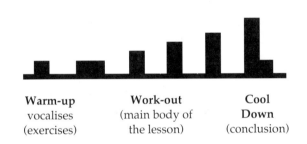

Warm-up	Work-out	Cool
vocalises	(main body of	**Down**
(exercises)	the lesson)	(conclusion)

(Graph reprinted from *Jubilate! A Newsletter for United Methodist Musicians*, No. 3, 1990)

The following suggestions are intended to spark the powers of your creative thinking.

1. Introduce and/or teach a song
   a) with a story or Bible verse
   b) through a listening activity (directed listening, listening for specific things, active use of the imagination)
   c) by clapping the rhythm of the words or by speaking rhythm words

   (ta, tee-tee, toe, tim-ree, tee-ree-tee-ree)

   d) by singing melodic fragments on sol-fa syllables or on neutral syllables such as "mah" or "loo"

e) by using drama—puppets, role playing, skits, and so on
f) through art work—teaching posters, flash cards, pictures and drawings, various types of song charts (such as a picture chart of the text, rhythm and melodic direction charts, and charts indicating the form of the song)
g) through games
h) through physical responses to melody and rhythm—dancing, marching, skipping, body ostinati such as clap-patschen-clap-patschen (*patschen* is a German word meaning to slap the legs or thighs), playing instruments (see **"Love of Instruments"** for more discussion on this topic)
i) by asking the children questions and engaging in dialogue about the song
j) by rote or by reading rhythm, sol-fa syllables, or staff notation

Encourage the children to involve their whole bodies in singing. As music educator Helen Kemp says, "Body, mind, spirit, voice, it takes the whole person to sing and rejoice."

Teach musical elements sequentially, beginning with the most basic and progressing to more complex ones. Some of these elements include:

- high/low, loud/soft, and fast/slow
- developing a feeling for the heartbeat (steady beat) of the music
- learning simple rhythms such as

ta ta tee-tee ta and tee-tee tee-tee ta rest

- recognizing basic intervals such as sol-mi, sol-la, sol-do
- recognizing basic patterns—phrases, form, same/different
- hearing and seeing the differences between steps and skips
- being able to read rhythms and melodies

Warm-ups and Vocal Production

The warm-up is just that—a time of warming up or awakening the singing voice. We know that a car engine runs better when it is warm. Likewise, the voice "runs" better when it has been prepared for singing. In the five or more minutes usually allotted for the warm-up, the children can sing throughout their ranges; get into their head voices; practice brief rhythms and melodies; fine-tune their group sound by listening to and blending with one another; practice vowel sounds and consonants; rehearse short, difficult melodic or rhythmic passages from songs they are learning; concentrate on the breathing apparatus; and get into good singing posture.

All this is possible in a few short minutes? Yes, *if* you have planned ahead. You must know what you wish to accomplish in the warm-up and lead the children through your plan.

Here are some suggestions for a warm-up session.

1. *Goal: to sing throughout the vocal range.*

Begin singing in the middle of the voice and expand upwards and downwards as the voice becomes more warmed-up. Encourage the children to keep their throats open and to produce a tone that feels "easy" and "relaxed," never pushed.

a) Sing five notes down (sol-fa-mi-re-do or mi-re-do-ti-la) on "mah," "me," "moh"

b) Staccato (short) triads: major (do-mi-sol-do-sol-mi-do) and minor (la-do-mi-la-mi-do-la); sing on sol-fa syllables or "ha," "ho," "he"

2. *Goal: to get into head voices.*

a) Siren: have the children make a siren sound, beginning on a low, indefinite pitch and going higher. Use the "ee" vowel for the lower pitches, and open the mouth wider as the notes rise in pitch. Let the "ee" vowel modify toward an "uh" sound. Let the children raise their arms over their heads as the "siren" ascends in pitch.

b) Indicate melodic movement with hand/arm motions (e.g., raising the arm over the head and lowering the arm to knee level) or draw a picture of melodic motion on the chalkboard or pad of newsprint.

3. *Goal: to practice brief rhythms and melodies.*

a) Echo-clap and echo-sing: the teacher or a child can initiate the short patterns.

b) Use rhythmic and melodic fragments from songs the children are learning. Sing these fragments on rhythm words, sol-fa syllables, and neutral vowel sounds.

4. *Goal: to blend and listen.*

a) Encourage the children to "listen to your neighbor." "If you can't hear your neighbor, you are probably singing too loud. When we sing as a group, no one voice should be heard above the others."

b) Sing simple music responses in dialogue with the children. This gives the singers a chance to sing solo and lets you hear how well they sing in tune and remember simple melodies. (See page 11 for **"Examples of Conversational Singing and Speaking."**)

5. *Goal: to practice vowel sounds and consonants.*

a) Sing this pattern on "father," "bubble," "pepper," "cookie."

b) Pick words with difficult sounds from the songs the children are learning.

6. *Goal: to concentrate on the breathing apparatus.*
   a) Ask the children to imagine that when they take in a breath to sing, they are "filling up a flat tire" around their middles.
   b) Practice panting like a dog on "ha," putting one finger in the belly button in order to feel the bounce of the breathing muscles.

7. *Goal: to maintain good singing posture.*
Images are very helpful when thinking about good singing posture.
   a) Discuss how correct singing posture is like an "oak tree." Our feet are like the roots planted deep in the ground. The feet should be several inches apart with one foot slightly ahead of the other. The children should feel "firmly rooted" to the floor yet able to wiggle their knees. The trunk of the body is like the straight trunk of the oak. Our head is like the leaf-covered branches.
   b) Picture your head as a "balloon filled with helium." Imagine that your spine is the "string attached to the balloon."
   c) Practice tension-relieving exercises such as rolling the shoulders frontward and backward.

Love of Instruments

Children love to play instruments. Instruments help children feel a sense of accomplishment, feel freer from inhibitions, think creatively, express themselves, and develop muscular coordination. In addition, playing instruments is just plain fun!

When considering the purchase of instruments, remember that it is much better to buy a few good instruments rather than a larger number of bad ones. Children need to learn the sound of high-quality instruments, not cheap toys. Many quality instruments are available at a reasonable cost. The following instruments will make suitable additions to any music program.

Unpitched Instruments:
- tambourine
- rhythm sticks
- drums (various sizes of hand drums, ethnic drums)
- wood blocks/tone blocks
- claves
- finger cymbals
- triangle
- cymbals

Pitched Instruments:
- resonator bells or tone chimes
- Orff instruments: glockenspiels, xylophones, metallophones
- autoharp
- recorders

Measuring Success

Success begins with you, the dedicated teacher and music leader. You can be successful if you:
- Set realistic goals. Choose goals that are appropriate for the age level with whom you work and for your unique situation.
- Choose music and plan music activities that will enable the children to achieve these goals.
- Evaluate the effectiveness of the music experiences, updating or revising your goals and teaching methods as necessary. If something doesn't work, decide whether to try it again, revise it, or eliminate it. Avoid blaming the children if a plan fails—evaluate instead!
- Assess your situation by asking questions such as:
   1. Are the children singing? Why or why not? What can I do to encourage them to sing?

2. Is participation high or low? What are the reasons?
3. What are the children learning through their musical involvement? Positive? Negative?
4. Do they enjoy making music? If the answer is "no" or "sometimes," what can I do to help the children have more positive music experiences?

The door of creative possibilities is open wide to you. Use your imagination to visualize your music situation as it is now and how you wish it to be. Envision new and exciting ways of engaging the children in the joy of music making. Pretend you are a child in the group you teach, picturing yourself actually participating in the music activities you lead. Discover what you, as a child, might gain from these activities. What would interest and delight you?

Let us help the children with whom we work explore the world of music, encouraging them to "Sing for Joy" to the Lord our God!

Helpful Resources

Children Sing His Praise, A Handbook for Children's Choir Directors, ed. Donald Rotermund. Concordia Publishing House, ISBN 0-570-01333-X.

Directing the Children's Choir, A Comprehensive Resource, Shirley W. McRae. Schirmer Books, ISBN 0-02-871785-6.

Handbook for Children's and Youth Choir Directors, Donald W. Roach. Choristers Guild, CGBK-45.

Lifeline for Children's Choir Directors, Jean Ashworth Bartle. Oxford University Press, ISBN 077-157250-6.

Of Primary Importance I and II, Helen Kemp. Choristers Guild, CGBK-50 and CGBK-54.

Our Heritage of Hymns and *Our Heritage of Hymns, Series II,* ed. Mary Nelson Keithahn. Choristers Guild, CGBK-43 and CGBK-49.

Quarter Notes: For Leaders of Music with Children, a quarterly magazine published by The United Methodist Publishing House.

Examples of Conversational
Singing and Speaking

Hello, What's Your Name?

For accompaniment with autoharp or guitar, use a C chord throughout, or double the melody on a keyboard instrument.

WORDS and MUSIC: Patricia Ann Meyers

© 1992 Cokesbury

Goodbye, Boys and Girls

WORDS and MUSIC: Nylea L. Butler-Moore

© 1993 Abingdon Press

I See a Friend of Jesus

WORDS and MUSIC: Suanne Williams-Whorl
© 1989 Graded Press

Welcome Someone Special

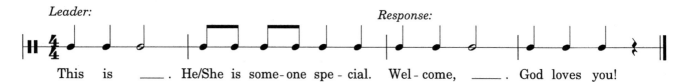

WORDS and MUSIC: Ron Anderson
© 1992 Cokesbury

The Invitation Game

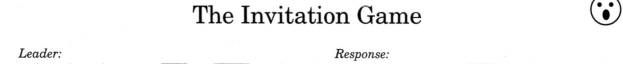

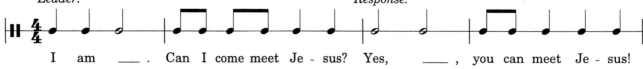

WORDS and MUSIC: Ron Anderson
© 1992 Cokesbury

A Guide to Spanish Pronunciation

Vowels:
A pronounced "ah"
E pronounced "eh"
I pronounced "ee"
O pronounced "oh"
U pronounced "oo"

Examples of clear vowels within words:
A E Í A—alegría
I E O—Cielo
A E O—cantemos
E E E—exprese
O E A O—soberano
O I A—gloria
A U O A—aurora
U E O—pueblo
U O—mundo
I A E—Israel
I O—Dios

Consonants where interference may come into play:
1. C—when followed by an A, O, or U, C is pronounced like a K; when followed by an I or E, C is pronounced like an S
2. H—no sound, as in himno, hizo, Hijo, hombre, hay
   Examples of words that are run together when there is an initial H: un himno, el hombre, su hermano, donde hay
3. CH—always a hard sound like in church, as in antorcha, dicho, bienhechora
4. J, GE, GI—like the English H, as in dejando, Jesús, lejana, ejércitos, Jerusalén, escoger, agita, gente
5. QUE, QUI—like the English K, as in que, quise, doquier
6. GUI—the U is silent and the G is hard, as in guia
7. LL, Y—stronger than the English Y (as in the word yonder), as in estrellas, semilla, ellos, orilla, aleluya
8. Ñ—like the "ni" in onion, as in pequeña, extraño
9. V—like the English B, as in nuevo, vio, venimos, vida

10. S, Z—like the English S in soap (never Z), as in gozo, tristeza, luz, feliz, Jesús, Jerusalén, hosana, masa
11. Initial R or middle double R—stronger than in English, requires two or three trills, as in regalo, rindo, tierra

Accents:
Usually the stress falls on the *next to last syllable* whenever the word ends in a vowel (A, E, I, O, U), N or S. It falls on the *last syllable* if the word ends in any consonant other than N or S. Whenever there is any deviation from these rules, you will see a written accent (').

Examples:
*can*ten (stress on next to last syllable—ends on N)
can*te*mos (stress on next to last syllable—ends on S)
re*ga*lo (stress on next to last syllable—ends on a vowel)
Se*ñor* (stress on last syllable—ends on R)
fe*liz* (stress on last syllable—ends on Z)
reci*én* (exception, accent mark denotes stress on last syllable)
Jes*ús* (exception, accent mark denotes stress on last syllable)
*cán*tico (exception, accent mark denotes stress on first syllable)
*dé*bil (exception, accent mark denotes stress on first syllable)

(Reprinted from *Church Music Workshop*, Vol. 3, No. 1)

Wisely Made!

WORDS: James Ritchie (refrain adapted from Psalm 104:24, *Good News Bible*)
MUSIC: James Ritchie; arr. by Timothy Edmonds

Refrain © 1989, 1992 Graded Press; stanzas © 1990 James Ritchie

Invite the children to go on a real or imaginary trip to the zoo. Let them list every animal they can think of. Add the animals mentioned in the song if they have not already been listed. Speak the words of the stanza in the triplet rhythm (1-2-3, 1-2-3), then learn the tune. Notice how the first, third, and fifth measures of the stanza are the same. The last two measures are just different enough to cause trouble. Sing each phrase and have the children echo. If you are called upon to present this piece in worship or at another occasion, invite the congregation or audience to sing along on "How wisely you made them, made them all."

(John Yarrington, reprinted from Spring 1992 *Quarter Notes*, p. 1)

GOD AND GOD'S WORLD
WORLD COMMUNITY

¿Quién Hace las Flores?
(Who Makes the Flowers?)

English Words:

1. Who makes the flowers? Our God.
2. Who makes the rain? Our God.
3. Who makes the seas? Our God.
4. Who makes the clouds? Our God.

WORDS: Clotilde F. Náñez
MUSIC: M. M. Ragsdale

Let the children play rhythm instruments as they sing this song.

Many and Great, O God

1. Man - y and great, O God, are thy things, Mak - er of
2. Grant un - to us com - mun - ion with thee, thou star a -

earth and sky. Thy hands have set the heav - ens with stars;
bid - ing one; come un - to us and dwell with us;

thy fin - gers spread the moun - tains and plains. Lo, at thy
with thee are found the gifts of life. Bless us with

word the wa - ters were formed; deep seas o - bey thy voice.
life that has no end, e - ter - nal life with thee.

Suggested Percussion

Sleigh bells   Big hand drum   Small hand drum

Dakota Words:

1. Wakantanka taku nitawa
   tankaya qa ota;
   mahpiya kin eyahnake ca,
   maka kin he duowanca,
   mniowanca sbeya wanke cin,
   hena oyakihi.

2. Nitawacin wasaka, wakan,
   on wawicahyaye;
   woyute qa wokoyake kin,
   woyatke ko iyacinyan,
   anpetu kin otoiyohi
   wawiyohiyaye.

WORDS: *Dakota Odowan: Dakota Hymns,* Hymn 141 by Joseph R. Renville; paraphrase by Philip Frazier
MUSIC: Trad. Dakota; arr. for percussion by Shirley W. McRae

Teach the children something about the people and culture of the Dakota nation. Explain that the text of this song reflects the Dakota people's love and respect for the "Maker of earth and sky" and for all of creation.

For the Beauty of the Earth

1. For the beau - ty of the earth, for the glo - ry of the skies,
2. For the beau - ty of each hour of the day and of the night,
3. For the joy of ear and eye, for the heart and mind's de - light,
4. For the joy of hu - man love, broth - er, sis - ter, par - ent, child,
5. For thy church, that ev - er - more lift - eth ho - ly hands a - bove,
6. For thy - self, best Gift Di - vine! to our race so free - ly given;

for the love which from our birth o - ver and a - round us lies:
hill and vale, and tree and flower, sun and moon, and stars of light:
for the mys - tic har - mo - ny link - ing sense to sound and sight:
friends on earth, and friends a - bove; for all gen - tle thoughts and mild:
of - fering up on ev - ery shore her pure sac - ri - fice of love:
for that great, great love of thine, peace on earth, and joy in heaven:

Lord of all, to thee we raise this our hymn of grate - ful praise.

WORDS: Folliot S. Pierpoint
MUSIC: Conrad Kocher
Arr. © 1964 Graded Press

17

God Made the Earth

1. God made the earth, God made the sea, all liv - ing things
2. God made the day, God made the night, sun, moon, and stars

made for you and me. Care for God's good earth each day,
giv - ing us great light. Shin - ing on the earth so fair which

give your thanks in ev - 'ry way. God made the earth, God saw that it was good.
God has left to our care.

Optional Handbells or Glockenspiel

Last time

Suggestions for singing:

> melody and bell–ostinato only
> melody, accompaniment, and bells
> melody and accompaniment

WORDS and MUSIC: Susan Eltringham (based on Genesis 1:10)
© 1993 Abingdon Press

He's Got the Whole World in His Hands

Other possible stanzas:
He's got the sun and the moon in his hands
He's got everybody here in his hands

WORDS and MUSIC: African American spiritual, arr. by Nylea L. Butler-Moore
Arr. © 1993 Abingdon Press

Use an inflatable, soft, or stuffed globe. Pass the globe (or ball if no globe is available) on the heart-beat (steady beat) of the song.

Hymn of Promise

1. In the bulb there is a flow - er; in the seed, an ap - ple tree;
2. There's a song in ev - ery si - lence, seek - ing word and mel - o - dy;
3. In our end is our be - gin - ning; in our time, in - fin - i - ty;

in co - coons, a hid - den prom - ise: but - ter - flies will soon be free!
there's a dawn in ev - ery dark - ness, bring - ing hope to you and me.
in our doubt there is be - liev - ing; in our life, e - ter - ni - ty.

In the cold and snow of win - ter there's a spring that waits to be,
From the past will come the fu - ture; what it holds, a mys - ter - y,
In our death, a res - ur - rec - tion; at the last, a vic - to - ry,

un - re - vealed un - til its sea - son, some - thing God a - lone can see.

WORDS and MUSIC: Natalie Sleeth
© 1986 Hope Publishing Co.

The Care the Eagle Gives Her Young

1. The care the ea - gle gives her young, safe
2. As when the time to ven - ture comes, she
3. And if we flut - ter help - less - ly, as

in her loft - y nest, is like the ten - der
stirs them out to flight, so we are pressed to
fledg - ling ea - gles fall, be - neath us lift God's

love of God for us made man - i - fest.
bold - ly try, to us strive for dar - ing height.
might - y wings to bear us, one and all.

WORDS: R. Deane Postlethwaite (based on Deuteronomy 32:11)
MUSIC: Jesse Seymour Irvine
Arr. © 1989 Graded Press

The Lord's My Shepherd

1. The Lord's my Shepherd, I'll not want;
   he makes me down to lie
   in pastures green; he leadeth me
   the quiet waters by.

2. My soul he doth restore again,
   and me to walk doth make
   within the paths of righteousness,
   e'en for his own name's sake.

3. Yea, though I walk in death's dark vale,
   yet will I fear no ill;
   for thou art with me, and thy rod
   and staff me comfort still.

4. My table thou hast furnished
   in presence of my foes;
   my head thou dost with oil anoint,
   and my cup overflows.

5. Goodness and mercy all my life
   shall surely follow me;
   and in God's house forevermore
   my dwelling place shall be.

WORDS: *Scottish Psalter* (Psalm 23)

Activity on page 22.

Discuss with the children how God cares for us much in the same way as an eagle cares for her young. If using the text, "The Lord Is My Shepherd," discuss how God cares for us much in the same way as a shepherd cares for the sheep.

LIFE OF JESUS

Lord of the Dance

1. "I danced in the morn-ing when the world was be-gun, and I danced in the moon and the stars and the sun, and I came down from heav-en and I danced on the earth. At Beth - le - hem I
2. "I danced for the scribe and the Phar - i - see, but they would not dance and they would not fol - low me; I danced for the fish - er - men, for James and John; they came to me and the
3. "I danced on the sab - bath when I cured the lame, the ho - ly peo - ple said it was a shame; they whipped and they stripped and they hung me high; and they left me there on a
4. "I danced on a Fri - day and the sky turned black; it's hard to dance with the dev - il on your back; they bur - ied my bod - y and they thought I'd gone, but I am the dance and I
5. "They cut me down and I leapt up high, I am the life that - 'll nev - er, nev - er die; I'll live in you if you'll live in me; I am the Lord of the

WORDS: Sydney Carter
MUSIC: 19th cent. Shaker tune; adapt. by Sydney Carter, harm. by Gary Alan Smith
© 1963, 1989 Galliard, Ltd.

22

Ask the children who is speaking in the text. Make sure they understand that Jesus is the "Lord of the dance" and that Jesus wants us to join in the "dance." Ask the children what kind of dance this is. For fun, have the children bunny hop to the recording of this song.

Allelu!

Al - le-lu! Al - le-lu! Ev-'ry-bod-y sing Al - le-lu! For the

Lord has ris - en, it is true: Ev - 'ry - bod-y sing Al - le - lu!

1. God said he would send his Son, al-le-lu, al - le-lu! to
2. Christ was born in Beth - le - hem, al- le-lu, al - le-lu!
3. Thir - ty years he walked the land, al- le-lu, al - le-lu! to
4. On the hard-wood of the cross, al-le-lu, al - le-lu! he
5. On the third day he did rise, al-le-lu, al - le-lu!
6. Now we too can live a-new, al-le-lu, al - le-lu!

and sal - va - tion would be won, al - le-lu - ia!
so that we would live a - gain, al-le-lu - ia!
all in need he lent his hand, al-le-lu - ia!
suf-fered and he died for us, al-le-lu - ia!
now he lives no more to die, al-le-lu - ia!
live in him need all we do, al-le-lu - ia!

WORDS and MUSIC: Ray Repp

A soloist may sing the verses and all respond with the refrain.

O Sing a Song of Bethlehem

1. O sing a song of Bethlehem, of shepherds watching there,
2. O sing a song of Nazareth, of sunny days of joy;
3. O sing a song of Galilee, of lake and woods and hill,
4. O sing a song of Calvary, its glory and dismay,

and of the news that came to them from angels in the air.
O sing of fragrant flowers' breath, and of the sinless Boy.
of him who walked upon the sea and bade the waves be still.
of him who hung upon the tree, and took our sins away.

The light that shone on Bethlehem fills all the world today;
For now the flowers of Nazareth in every heart may grow;
For though like waves on Galilee, dark seas of trouble roll,
For he who died on Calvary is risen from the grave,

of Jesus' birth and peace on earth the angels sing alway.
now spreads the fame of his dear name on all the winds that blow.
when faith has heard the Master's word, falls peace upon the soul.
and Christ, our Lord, by heaven adored, is mighty now to save.

WORDS: Louis F. Benson
MUSIC: English melody; arr. by Ralph Vaughan Williams

Teach the children about Ralph Vaughan Williams and his contributions to the music of the church.

Jesus, Our Friend

WORDS and MUSIC: Jenni Douglas

Ask the children what they can do to be a friend and to help others. Memorize the Bible verse, "A friend loves at all times" (Proverbs 17:17 NRSV).

When Jesus the Healer Passed Through Galilee

1. When Je - sus the heal - er passed through Gal - i - lee,
2. A par - a - lyzed man was let down through a roof.
3. The death of his daugh - ter caused Jai - rus to weep.
4. When blind Bar - ti - mae - us cried out to the Lord,
5. The lep - ers were healed and the de - mons cast out.

Heal us, heal us to - day!

the deaf came to hear and the
His sins were for - giv - en, his
The Lord took her hand, and he
His faith made him whole and his
A bent wo - man straight - ened to

blind came to see.
walk - ing the proof.
raised her from sleep.
sight was re - stored.
laugh and to shout.

Heal us, Lord Je - sus!

6. The twelve were commissioned and sent out in twos
   Heal us, heal us today!
   to make the sick whole and to spread the good news.
   Heal us, Lord Jesus!

7. There's still so much sickness and suffering today.
   Heal us, heal us today!
   We gather together for healing and pray:
   Heal us, Lord Jesus!

WORDS and MUSIC: Peter D. Smith
© 1979 Stainer and Bell, Ltd.

Act out the text of this hymn with a leader singing the verses and the group singing the responses, "Heal us, heal us today!" and "Heal us, Lord Jesus!" You may teach the stanzas separately to coincide with the teaching of specific Bible stories.

Tell Me, Tell Me

1. Tell me, tell me have you heard? To
2. fol - low Je - sus they all came.
5. Je - sus called and these twelve came.
6. Je - sus says, "Come fol - low, too."

Tell me, tell me have you heard of twelve dis - ci - ples who
fol - low Je - sus they all came. Now let us call each
Je - sus called and these twelve came. Now you know each
Je - sus says, "Come fol - low, too." Je - sus needs dis - ci - ples, and

spread God's word. Of twelve dis - ci - ples who spread God's word. To
one by name. Now let us call each one by name.
one by name. Now you know each one by name.
he needs you! Je - sus needs dis - ci - ples, and he needs you!

WORDS: Lesa Piper
MUSIC: Traditional; arr. by Lesa Piper

Ostinati Accompaniment

Orff Instruments (xylophones) or tone chimes

Rhythm Instruments

List on a poster the names of the twelve disciples in the order in which they occur in the song. The leader/response style offers the children an opportunity to have a solo or to lead. Maintain a steady beat throughout with rhythm instruments. Orff instruments and tone chimes serve to enrich the piano accompaniment.

(Lesa Piper, reprinted from *VBS 1991 Music and Activities Manual*, p. 1)

Amen

1. See the lit-tle ba - by _____
2. See him in the tem - ple _____
3. Je - sus is my Sav - ior, _____

1. ly - ing in a man - ger _____ one Christ-mas morn - ing. _
2. talk - ing to the eld - ers. _____ How they mar - veled at his wis - dom. _
3. Je - sus died to save us, _____ And he rose on Eas - ter. _

All voices may repeat the first "Amens" after stanza 3.

WORDS and MUSIC: African American spiritual; harm. by J. Jefferson Cleveland and Verolga Nix;
   adapt. by Nylea L. Butler-Moore

Harm. © 1980 Abingdon Press; adapt. © 1993 Abingdon Press

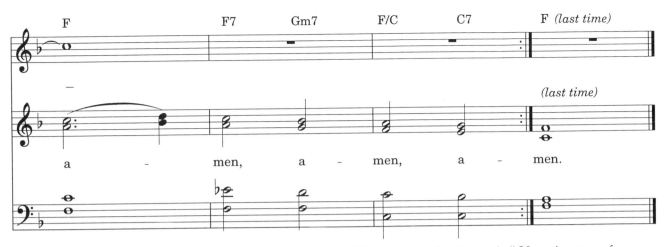

The teacher or a soloist may sing the verses and the children sing the "amen's." Use pictures of Jesus as a baby and as a boy in the temple. You may teach only one verse at a time to coincide with the teaching of a particular Bible story.

THE CHURCH

We Are Your Church, O God

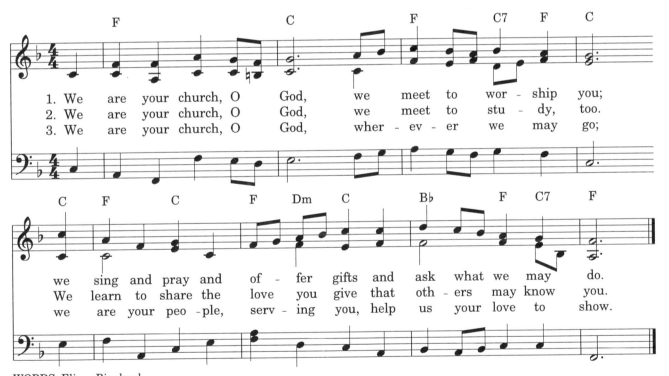

1. We are your church, O God, we meet to wor - ship you;
2. We are your church, O God, we meet to stu - dy, too.
3. We are your church, O God, wher - ev - er we may go;

we sing and pray and of - fer gifts and ask what we may do.
We learn to share the love you give that oth - ers may know you.
we are your peo - ple, serv - ing you, help us your love to show.

WORDS: Elinor Ringland
MUSIC: Aaron Williams, *The New Universal Psalmodist*
Words © 1966 Graded Press; arr. © 1964 Graded Press

Visit the sanctuary and discuss what we do in the worship service. What reminders do we have about singing, praying, and offering gifts? Pantomime the words: "sing"—hands on each side of mouth or a gesture from chin forward with open hand; "pray"—fold hands in prayer; "offer gifts"—hands spread, palms up; "share"—take hold of another's hand; "serving"—hands spread, palms up; "help"—fold hands in prayer.

(Reprinted from *VBS 1987 Music and Activities Manual*, p. 13)

The Church Is Wherever God's People Are Praising

Bells, Orff, etc.

Soprano instrument

1. The church is wher-ev-er God's peo-ple are prais-ing,
2. The church is wher-ev-er God's peo-ple are help-ing,

Organ pedal, low bells, Orff, etc.

sing-ing their thanks for joy on this day. The church is wher-ev-er dis-
car-ing for neigh-bors in sick-ness and need. The church is wher-ev-er God's

ci-ples of Je-sus re-mem-ber his sto-ry and walk in his way.
peo-ple are shar-ing the words of the Bi-ble in gift and in deed.

* Finger cymbal

WORDS: Carol Rose Ikeler
MUSIC: Traditional Cornish melody; arr. by Jane Marshall

Words copyright © 1963, 1991 W. L. Jenkins, from *Songs and Hymns for Primary Children*. Used by permission of The Westminster / John Knox Press
Arr. © 1982 Jane Marshall

This text by Carol Rose Ikeler presents the perfect opportunity for children to learn that the church is not just a building. Have them find the different activities of the church in the text—praising, singing, helping, caring, sharing. Ask them where they see this happening in their church, and have them discuss how they can be a part of these activities. On a chart, list the activities of the church and encourage the children to practice a different one each day of the week.

If you do not have Orff instruments or if you would prefer to accompany this song with the piano, simply play the two lowest staves. (Brett A. Edler, reprinted from Winter 1992–93 *Quarter Notes*, p. 2)

Christian, Welcome

WORDS and MUSIC: James Ritchie
© 1986 James Ritchie

This piece is to be sung as a response to baptism. Talk with the children about baptism and its significance to the individual and the church. Remind them that they were given their names when they were born so that people would know who they are. When people are baptized, the name "Christian" becomes part of who they are. The baptized person is part of a wonderful fellowship that includes people of all times and places. Read the words and discuss their meaning with the children.

(Janeal Krehbiel, reprinted from Winter 1990–91 *Quarter Notes*, p. 8)

The Bread of Life for All Is Broken

WORDS: Timothy Tingfang Lew; trans. by Walter Reginald Oxenham Taylor; phonetic transcription from the Chinese by I-to Loh
MUSIC: Su Yin-Lan; harm. by Robert C. Bennett
Phonetic transcription © 1989 The United Methodist Publishing House; harm. © 1989 The United Methodist Publishing House

Use this song during a study of Holy Communion or in a worship service in which Communion is served. Discuss the significance of the Lord's Supper with the children. Teach them the Chinese text.

"Let Us Talents and Tongues Employ" uses a Communion text by Fred Kaan, an important twentieth-century hymn writer. Ask the children what we do during Communion. What's another phrase we might use for this act of worship? (the Lord's Supper). Discuss this "supper" in which we are invited to the table to join in remembering what Christ has done for us and then are sent into the world in service. Put key words ("talents," "tongues," "bread," "wine," "breathe," "Word," "tone," "bless," and "Immanuel") on sheets of paper to display around the room. Explain these words to the children. Keep the words posted as a way of reinforcing the ideas. Add maracas, finger cymbals, and drums if available. (John Yarrington, reprinted from Spring 1992 *Quarter Notes*, p. 2)

Let Us Talents and Tongues Employ

1. Let us tal - ents and tongues em - ploy, reach - ing out with a shout of joy: bread is bro - ken, the wine is poured, Christ is spo - ken and seen and heard.
2. Christ is a - ble to make us one, at his ta - ble he sets the tone, teach - ing peo - ple to live to bless, love in word and in deed ex - press.
3. Je - sus calls us in, sends us out bear - ing fruit in a world of doubt, gives us love to tell, bread to share: God (Im - man - u - el) ev - ery - where!

Refrain

Je - sus lives a - gain, earth can breathe a - gain, pass the Word a - round: loaves a - bound!

WORDS: Fred Kaan
MUSIC: Jamaican Folk Song; adapt. by Doreen Potter
© 1975 Hope Publishing Co.

Activity on page 34.

Pues Si Vivimos
(When We Are Living)

WORDS: Stanza 1 anonymous, trans. by Elise S. Eslinger; stanzas 2, 3, 4 Roberto Escamilla, trans. by George Lockwood
MUSIC: Trad. Spanish melody; harm. from *Celebremos*

Trans. © 1989 The United Methodist Publishing House; Spanish trans. stanzas 2, 3, 4 used by permission

Discuss what it means to belong to God. Encourage the children to memorize Romans 14:8. Sing at least one or more stanzas in Spanish. (See "A Guide to Spanish Pronunciation" on page 13.)

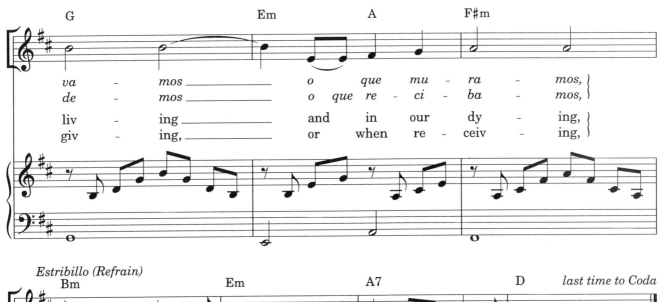

vamos _____ o que muramos, }
demos _____ o que recibamos, }
living _____ and in our dying, }
giving, _____ or when receiving, }

Estribillo (Refrain)

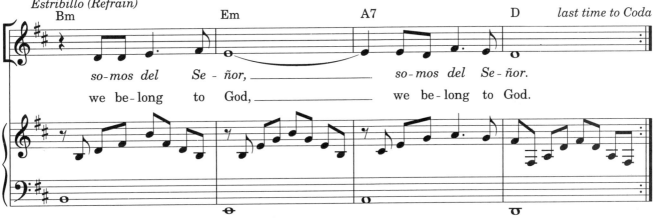

last time to Coda

so-mos del Se-ñor, _____ so-mos del Se-ñor.
we be-long to God, _____ we be-long to God.

Coda (Solamente la última vez)

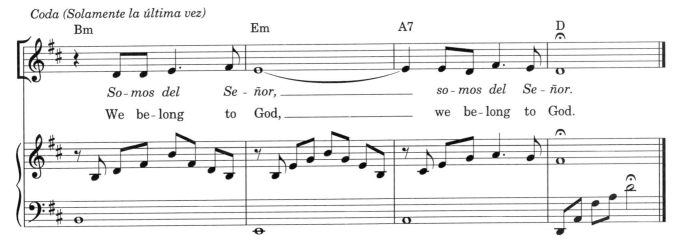

So-mos del Se-ñor, _____ so-mos del Se-ñor.
We be-long to God, _____ we be-long to God.

3. En la tristeza y en el dolor,
   en la belleza y en el amor,
   sea que suframos o que gocemos,
   Estribillo

4. En este mundo, hemos de encontrar
   gente que llora y sin consolar.
   Sea que ayudemos o que alimentemos,
   Estribillo

3. 'Mid times of sorrow and in times of pain,
   when sensing beauty or in love's embrace,
   whether we suffer, or sing rejoicing,
   Refrain

4. Across this wide world, we shall always find
   those who are crying with no peace of mind,
   but when we help them, or when we feed them,
   Refrain

I Sing a Song of the Saints of God

WORDS: Lesbia Scott
MUSIC: John H. Hopkins, Jr.

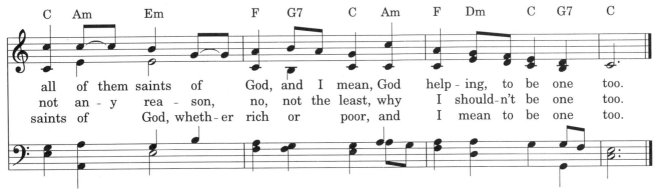

all of them saints of God, and I mean, God help-ing, to be one too.
not an-y rea-son, no, not the least, why I should-n't be one too.
saints of God, wheth-er rich or poor, and I mean to be one too.

This popular hymn is excellent for use when teaching about saints. Let the children choose a particular saint in the song, such as "one was a doctor," or "one was a priest," and have the children stand when their saint is mentioned. The children could also pretend to be one of these saints and improvise short skits about them. If your class or church plans to have a Halloween or All Saints' party, ask the children to dress up as one of the saints in the song. The children could also process in costume and lead an opening processional for worship while the congregation sings this hymn.

Prepare the Way
(Introit for Advent)

CHRISTIAN YEAR
BIBLE VERSES AND STORIES

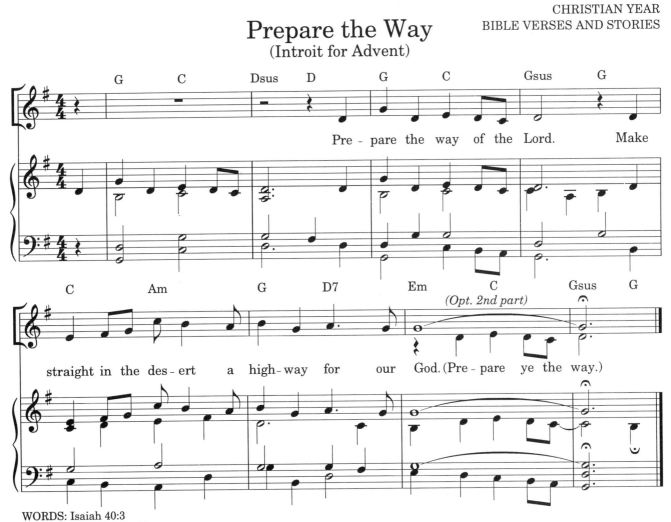

Pre-pare the way of the Lord. Make straight in the des-ert a high-way for our God. (Pre-pare ye the way.)

WORDS: Isaiah 40:3
MUSIC: Gary Alan Smith

This song makes a good Introit or Call to Worship that can be used during the four Sundays of Advent. Let the children locate Isaiah 40:3 in their Bibles, and point out to them that this verse is the text of the song.

Advent Candle Song

Light one can - dle: Christ is com - ing, Christ, the Hope of the world.
Light two can - dles: Christ is com - ing, Christ, the Way of the world.
Light three can - dles: Christ is com - ing, Christ, the Joy of the world.
Light four can - dles: Christ is com - ing, Christ, the Peace of the world.
Light the white one: Christ is born, Christ, the Light of the world.

Light one can - dle: Christ is com - ing, Christ is com - ing soon!
Light two can - dles: Christ is com - ing, Christ is com - ing soon!
Light three can - dles: Christ is com - ing, Christ is com - ing soon!
Light four can - dles: Christ is com - ing, Christ is com - ing soon!
Light the white one: Christ is born, Christ is born to - day!

May be sung as a 2-part round.

(night)

Canon may be doubled by keyboard

Ostinati for Handbells or Orff Instruments

Pattern 1

Ending

Pattern 2

L.V.

Ending

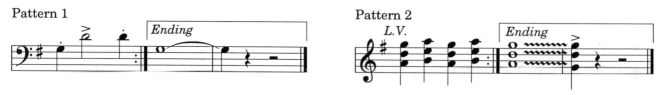

WORDS and MUSIC: Sally Ahner
© 1992 Abingdon Press

This song can be used during the four Sundays of Advent. It is most appropriately sung following the lighting of the Advent wreath.

Advent Is the Season
(A Song of the Christian Year)

1. Ad - vent is the sea - son of wait - ing for Mes - si - ah,
2. Christ - mas is the sea - son of wel - com - ing the Sav - ior,
3. E - piph - a - ny is the sea - son we think a - bout the Ma - gi, the
4. Lent is the sea - son of pray - ing for for - give - ness,
5. Eas - ter is the sea - son of great - est joy and glad - ness!
6. Pen - te - cost is the sea - son the Church came in - to be - ing.

light - ing Ad - vent can - dles, and know - ing Christ is near. We
Je - sus in a man - ger, a babe of poor - est birth. We
bright - ly shin - ing star, and the gifts fit for a King, Christ's
grow - ing as dis - ci - ples, and giv - ing to the poor. We
Je - sus is a - live! No long - er is he dead! The
It was born the day that the Ho - ly Spir - it came. The

hear the words of proph - ets spo - ken to the peo - ple, "Pre -
think a - bout the shep - herds and the host of an - gels
bap - ti - sm by John, the mir - a - cle at Ca - na. "E -
think of Je - sus' life, his fast - ing in the des - sert, the
stone was rolled a - way from the tomb where he was bur - ied.
Word of God was preached to man - y diff - 'rent peo - ples.

pare the way of God. Christ will soon be here."
prais - ing God and say - ing, "Peace to all on earth."
man - u - el is with us," gifts of praise we bring.
pain - ful cru - ci - fix - ion he knew he must en - dure.
"Je - sus is not here! He has ris - en as he said."
Thou - sands in the crowd be - lieved on Je - sus' name.

WORDS and MUSIC: Nylea L. Butler-Moore

Activity on page 42.

You may teach the entire song or one stanza at a time to coincide with a particular season of the Christian year. Let the children make simple banners or draw pictures of Christian symbols (such as the Advent wreath, the shepherds' staffs, the star of Epiphany, the Lenten crown of thorns, the butter-fly of Easter, the Pentecost tongues of flame), and display these in the classroom or in the sanctuary.

CHRISTIAN YEAR
WORLD COMMUNITY

That Boy-Child of Mary

WORDS: Tom Colvin (based on Luke 2:7)
MUSIC: Trad. Malawi melody; adapt. by Tom Colvin

The inner stanzas could easily be sung by a soloist with the children singing the refrain. Or, consider combinations of alternating between a soloist and the entire group. Since the melody of this song comes from Malawi, teach the children something about the country and the people who live there.

Niño Lindo
(Child So Lovely)

WORDS: Trad. Venezuelan; trans. by George Lockwood
MUSIC: Trad. Venezuelan melody

Trans. © 1989 The United Methodist Publishing House

This hauntingly beautiful music has many possible uses during the Christmas season. The refrain can be a Communion hymn or a response when gifts of food for the needy are brought forward. Study Christmas in Venezuela and teach the Spanish text. Guitar accompaniment would be most effective. (John W. Semingson, reprinted from Fall 1991 *Quarter Notes*, p. 6)

43

Gentle Mary Laid Her Child

1. Gen-tle Ma-ry laid her child   low-ly in a man - ger;
2. An-gels sang a-bout his birth,   wise men sought and found him;
3. Gen-tle Ma-ry laid her child   low-ly in a man - ger;

there he lay, the un-de-filed,   to the world a stran - ger.
heav-en's star shone bright-ly forth, glo-ry all a-round him.
he is still the un-de-filed,   but no more a stran - ger.

Such a babe in such a place,   can he be the Sav - ior?
Shep-herds saw the won-drous sight, heard the an-gels sing - ing;
Son of God, of hum-ble birth,   beau-ti-ful the sto - ry;

Ask the saved of all the race   who have found his fa - vor.
all the plains were lit that night; all the hills were ring - ing.
praise his name in all the earth; hail the King of glo - ry.

WORDS: Joseph S. Cook
MUSIC: "Tempus Adest Floridum" from *Piae Cantiones;* arr. based on harm. by Sir Ernest MacMillan
Arr. © 1967 Graded Press

Make sure the children understand the basic meaning of the text. Discuss the words, "undefiled" and "saved of all the race."

Bring a Torch, Jeannette, Isabella

(Un Flambeau, Jeannette, Isabelle)

1. Bring a torch, Jean-nette, Is-a-bel-la! Bring a torch, to the
cra-dle run. It is Je-sus, good folk of the vil-lage; Christ is
born and Ma-ry's call-ing: Ah! ah! beau-ti-ful is the
moth-er. Ah! ah! beau-ti-ful is the Child!_____

2. It is wrong when the ba-by is sleep-ing, it is wrong to
speak so loud. Si-lence now as you come near the cra-dle lest you a-
wak-en lit-tle Je-sus. Ah! ah! beau-ti-ful is the
moth-er. Ah! ah! beau-ti-ful is the Child!_____

3. Soft-ly now come in-to the sta-ble, soft-ly now for a
mo-ment come. Look and see how charm-ing is Je-sus, how he is
fair, his cheeks are ro-sy. Ah! ah! beau-ti-ful is the
moth-er. Ah! ah! beau-ti-ful is the Child!_____

WORDS: Traditional French text; trans. by Edward Cuthbert Nunn
MUSIC: Provençal Carol
Arr. © 1965 Graded Press

Optional French text to stanza one:

1. Un flambeau, Jeannette, Isabelle,
un flambeau, courons au berceau!
C'est Jésus, bonnes gens du hameau,
le Christ est né, Marie appelle,
Ah! ah! que la mère est belle,
Ah! ah! que l'Enfant est beau!

Act out the scene at the manger. Celebrating winter religious festivals with the carrying of torches is an old custom. The ancient Jews carried torches as part of their celebration of the Festival of Lights or Hanukkah.

Rock-a-Bye, My Dear Little Boy

1. Rock - a - bye, my dear lit - tle boy,
dear lit - tle boy, won - der of won - ders, my bless - ing and joy;
slum - ber as I gen - tly hold you, let my ten - der
love en - fold you; gift of God to me and the world,
here in my arms lies so peace - ful - ly curled.

2. Lit - tle Je - sus, In - fant Di - vine,
In - fant Di - vine, one with the Fa - ther, yet born to be mine;
as I rock you calm - ly sleep - ing, an - gel guards their
watch are keep - ing; pre - cious child, one day we shall see
what love has des - tined for you and for me.

WORDS: Czech carol; trans. by Jaroslav J. Vajda
MUSIC: Czech carol; melody collected by Martin Shaw

Remind the children that this Czech carol is a lullaby. Even the name of the tune is ROCKING. Encourage the children to imagine Mary singing this lullaby as she gently rocks her new baby boy, Jesus.

On Christmas Night

* Chords are for the key of D.

WORDS: Adapted from Luke 2:10-11
MUSIC: Traditional English Carol; arr. by Ralph Vaughan Williams

Arr. © 1986 Graded Press

The "leader/all" designation makes this song easy to learn, and the "leader" part could be sung by a teacher or a child soloist. Consider teaching the children about Ralph Vaughan Williams and his contributions to the music of the church.

Long, Long Ago

1. Winds through the ol - ive trees
2. Sheep on the hill - side lay
4. For in a man - ger bed,

soft - ly did blow, 'round lit - tle Beth - le - hem
whi - ter than snow; shep - herds were watch - ing them
cra - dled we know, Christ came to Beth - le - hem

long, long a - go.
long, long a - go.
long, long a -

*2nd part on stanzas 2, 3, and 4 optional

WORDS: Anonymous
MUSIC: Gary Alan Smith

© 1980 Hope Publishing Co.

Dakota Nativity

Rhythm Bells or Hand Drum

1. I - cy winds blew with might on the plains that win - ter night.
2. Three brave chiefs crossed the snow bear - ing pelts of buf - fa - lo:

Stood a star, from a - far, shin - ing on that ti - pi. *
gifts to keep Je - sus warm, sleep - ing in that ti - pi.

8vb

* *Dakota spelling*

WORDS and MUSIC: Dadee Reilly
© 1990 Dadee Reilly

Form a Native American nativity scene as this song progresses. Keep props and costuming uncomplicated so as not to interfere with the simplicity of the music and the text. Let the children play-act the nativity scene in a worship service or for other children's classes. Teach the young children the two "Come now, come and see" sections and have them sing along. Let them beat hand drums or oatmeal box drums in rhythm, accenting the first beat.

(Patty Clark, reprinted from Fall 1992 *Quarter Notes*, p. 3)

He Is Born

(Il Est Né)

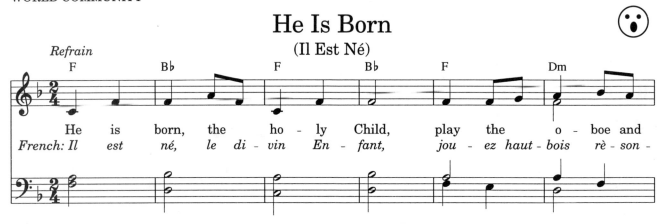

He is born, the ho - ly Child, play the o - boe and

French: Il est né, le di - vin En - fant, jou - ez haut - bois rè - son -

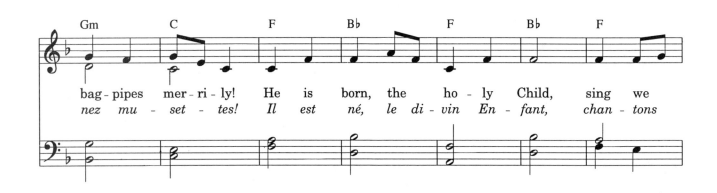

bag - pipes mer - ri - ly! He is born, the ho - ly Child, sing we

nez mu - set - tes! Il est né, le di - vin En - fant, chan - tons

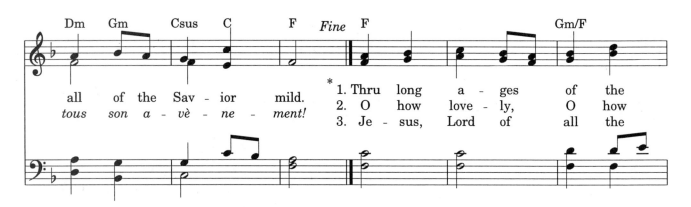

all of the Sav - ior mild.   *1. Thru long a - ges of the

tous son a - vè - ne - ment!   2. O how love - ly, O how

                                  3. Je - sus, Lord of all the

* *Stanzas may be sung in two parts.*

WORDS: Trad. 19th cent. French carol; trans. anonymous
MUSIC: 18th cent. French carol; harm. by Carlton R. Young

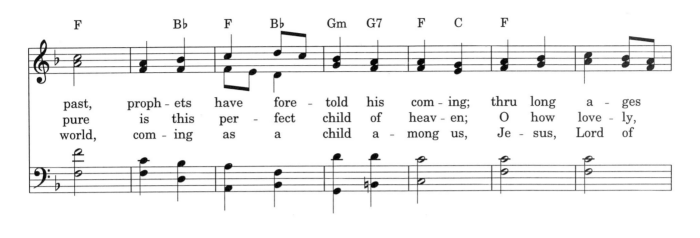

past, proph - ets have fore - told his com - ing; thru long a - ges
pure is this per - fect child of heav - en; O how love - ly,
world, com - ing as a child a - mong us, Je - sus, Lord of

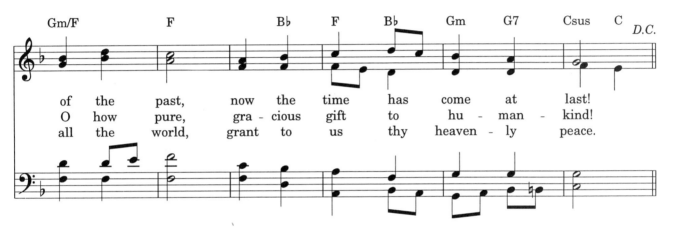

of the past, now the time has come at last!
O how pure, gra - cious gift to hu - man - kind!
all the world, grant to us thy heaven - ly peace.

Learn the French version of the refrain and alternate singing it in French and English. A soloist or the entire group could sing the stanzas. Discuss the prophets who "foretold his coming" and their message of the coming of Messiah. Make sure the children know what an oboe and bagpipes look and sound like.

Arise, Shine

WORDS: Isaiah 60:1
MUSIC: Gary Alan Smith

© 1990 Gamut Music Productions

Discuss the Epiphany symbol of the star and why the coming of Messiah is symbolized by a star or light. Let the children look up Isaiah 60:1 in their Bibles, and point out to them that this verse is the text of the song.

De Tierra Lejana Venimos
(From a Distant Home)

1. De-tie-rra le-ja - na ve-ni-mos a ver-te,
2. Al re-cién na-ci - do que es Rey de los re - yes,

1. From a dis-tant home the Sav-ior we come seek-ing,
2. Glow-ing gold I bring the new-born babe so ho - ly,

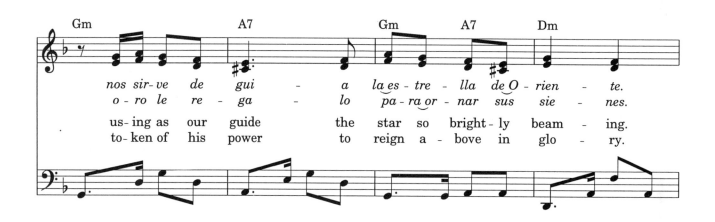

nos sir-ve de gui - a la es-tre - lla de O-rien - te.
o-ro le re-ga - lo pa-ra or-nar sus sie - nes.

us-ing as our guide the star so bright-ly beam - ing.
to-ken of his power to reign a-bove in glo - ry.

Estribillo (Refrain)

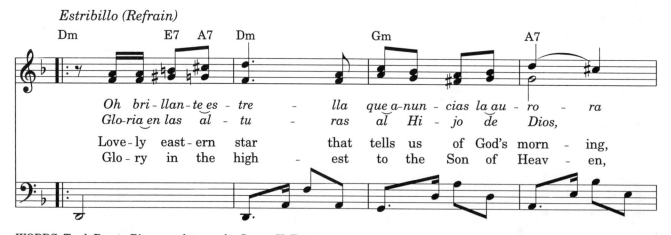

Oh bri-llan-te es-tre - lla que a-nun-cias la au-ro - ra
Glo-ria en las al-tu - ras al Hi-jo de Dios,

Love-ly east-ern star that tells us of God's morn-ing,
Glo-ry in the high - est to the Son of Heav-en,

WORDS: Trad. Puerto Rican carol; trans. by George K. Evans
MUSIC: Trad. Puerto Rican carol

no nos fal - te nun - ca tu luz bien - he - cho - ra.
Glo - ria en las al - tu - ras

heav-en's won-drous light, O nev - er cease thy shin - ing!
and up - on the earth be

y en la tie - rra a - mor. _____

peace and love to all. _____

3. Come es Dios el Niño le regalo incienso,
   perfume con alma que sube hasta el cielo.
   Estribillo

4. Al Niño del cielo que bajó a la tierra,
   le regalo mirra que inspira tristeza.
   Estribillo

3. Frankincense I bring the child of God's own choosing,
   token of our prayers to heaven ever rising.
   Refrain

4. Bitter myrrh have I to give the infant Jesus,
   token of the pain that he will bear to save us.
   Refrain

This lively Puerto Rican carol is a good Epiphany alternative to "We Three Kings." Let the children play rhythm instruments as they sing this song.

When Jesus Came to Jerusalem

When Jesus came to Jerusalem the children stood along the way { wav-ing palm branch-es, wav-ing / mak-ing room for Him, mak-ing } { palm branch-es / room for Him } for their Lord and King. Sing Ho- san - na, sing Ho-san - na to the Lord and King!

WORDS and MUSIC: John Erickson
© 1975 Graded Press

This song could be used on Palm Sunday as an Introit (Call to Worship) for both young and elementary-age children. Let the young children join in the singing of "Sing Hosanna." All the children could process with palm branches as they sing the song.

Hosanna

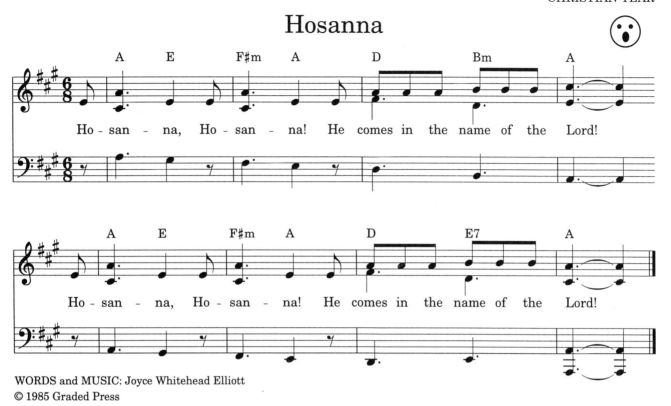

WORDS and MUSIC: Joyce Whitehead Elliott
© 1985 Graded Press

Help the children to correctly pronounce "Ho-SAH-nah." Finger cymbals and hand drum accompaniment will add to the rhythmic interest.

(Brett A. Edler, reprinted from Winter 1992–93 *Quarter Notes*, p. 1)

Here is a simple refrain that would work well as a processional following the reading of the Palm Sunday narrative. Instruct the children to repeat the refrain as they proceed down the aisle. This procession should feel festive with palms waving.

(Dan Stokes, reprinted from Winter 1991–92 *Quarter Notes*, p. 7)

Christ Is Risen

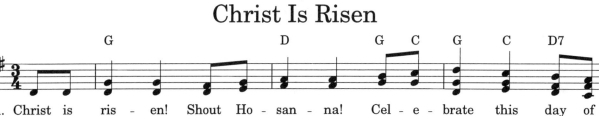

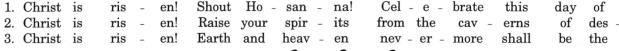

1. Christ is ris - en! Shout Ho - san - na! Cel - e - brate this day of
2. Christ is ris - en! Raise your spir - its from the cav - erns of des -
3. Christ is ris - en! Earth and heav - en nev - er - more shall be the

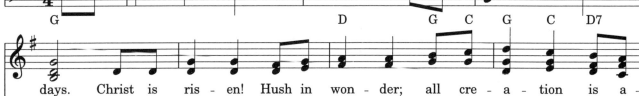

days. Christ is ris - en! Hush in won - der; all cre - a - tion is a -
pair. Walk with glad - ness in the morn - ing. See what love can do and
same. Break the bread of new cre - a - tion where the world is still in

mazed. In the de - sert all - sur - round - ing, see, a spread - ing tree has
dare. Drink the wine of res - ur - rec - tion, not a ser - vant, but a
pain. Tell its grim, de - mon - ic cho - rus: "Christ is ris - en! Get you

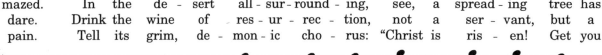

grown. Heal - ing leaves of grace a - bound - ing bring a taste of love un - known.
friend; Je - sus is our strong com - pan - ion. Joy and peace shall nev - er end.
gone!" God the First and Last is with us. Sing Ho - san - na ev - ery - one!

WORDS: Brian Wren
MUSIC: Polish carol; arr. by Edith M. G. Reed; harm. by Austin C. Lovelace
Words © 1986 Hope Publishing Co.; harm. © 1965 Abingdon Press

Use the words "Infant Holy, Infant Lowly" for Christmas and "Christ Is Risen" for Easter. Teach the children something about Poland and the people who live there. Also, consider teaching the children something about Brian Wren, the author of the "Christ Is Risen" text and an important twentieth-century hymnist.

Infant Holy, Infant Lowly

1. Infant holy, infant lowly, for his bed a cattle stall;
   oxen lowing, little knowing, Christ the babe is Lord of all.
   Swift are winging angels singing, noels ringing, tidings bringing;
   Christ the babe is Lord of all.

2. Flocks were sleeping, shepherds keeping vigil till the morning new
   saw the glory, heard the story, tidings of a gospel true.
   Thus rejoicing, free from sorrow, praises voicing, greet the morrow:
   Christ the babe was born for you.

WORDS: Polish carol, trans. by Edith M. G. Reed

Come, Holy Spirit, Heavenly Dove

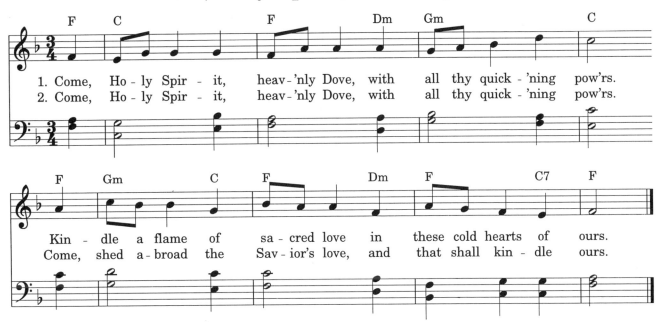

1. Come, Ho - ly Spir - it, heav - 'nly Dove, with all thy quick - 'ning pow'rs.
2. Come, Ho - ly Spir - it, heav - 'nly Dove, with all thy quick - 'ning pow'rs.

Kin - dle a flame of sa - cred love in these cold hearts of ours.
Come, shed a - broad the Sav - ior's love, and that shall kin - dle ours.

WORDS: Isaac Watts
MUSIC: USA campmeeting melody

Consider teaching this hymn in conjunction with the story of Pentecost found in Acts 2. Discuss the birth of the church and images/symbols used to represent the Holy Spirit.

Spirit of the Living God

WORDS: Daniel Iverson
MUSIC: Daniel Iverson

When introduced by flute, this familiar prayer chorus is especially beautiful and meditative. The accompaniment should be played softly and gently. Having the children softly hum a verse before singing will help them sense a spirit of quiet reverence. This selection serves as a meaningful call to prayer. For choir directors, here is a wonderful opportunity to teach a beginning lesson in musical form. Ask the children to find the phrases that are alike (1, 2, and 4), then identify the form as A-A-B-A.

(Dan Stokes, reprinted from Winter 1991–92 *Quarter Notes*, p. 7)

D-I-S-C-I-P-L-E-S

WORDS and MUSIC: James Ritchie; arr. by Timothy Edmonds

© 1990 Graded Press

Prepare a large piece of cloth or paper. Place the letters D, I, S, C, I, P, L, E, S on separate cards with velcro or tape on the back. Ask children to add the appropriate letter to the paper or cloth as the song is sung. Use a triangle or finger cymbals to enhance the two places where singers are to clap.

(Lesa Piper, reprinted from *VBS 1991 Music and Activities Manual*, p. 1)

Come! Come! Everybody Worship!

WORDS and MUSIC: Natalie Sleeth; Spanish trans. by Mary Lou Santillán-Baert

© 1991 Cokesbury

This is a good opening theme song or Call to Worship. Teach the children the following hand motions to use as they sing the refrain:

1. "Come! Come!" Use an inviting gesture.
2. "With a prayer." Fold hands in prayer position.
3. "Or song of praise." Arms outstretched, hands open.

1. "Come! Come!" Use inviting gesture again.
2. "Worship God always!" Repeat prayer position.

(John Yarrington, reprinted from Spring 1992 *Quarter Notes*, p. 2)

What God Requires

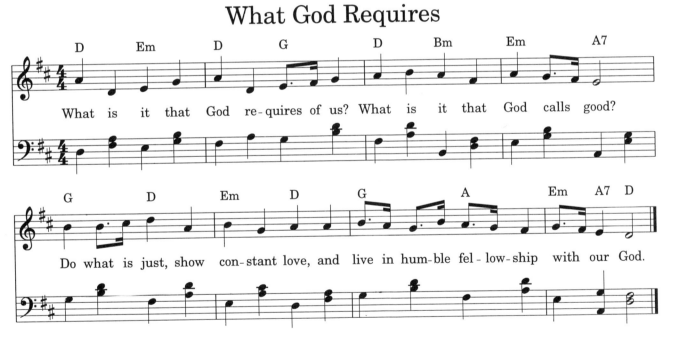

WORDS: Based on Micah 6:8
MUSIC: James Ritchie
Music © 1989 Graded Press

This adaptation of Micah 6:8 offers a good way for children to commit this verse to memory. Discuss with the children the concept of justice to make sure that they have an understanding of what it means to "do justice." Use a Bible story such as the Good Samaritan (Luke 10:29-37) as an example.

(Jerry M. Hollis, reprinted from Spring 1990 *Quarter Notes*, p. 7)

Love God with Your Heart

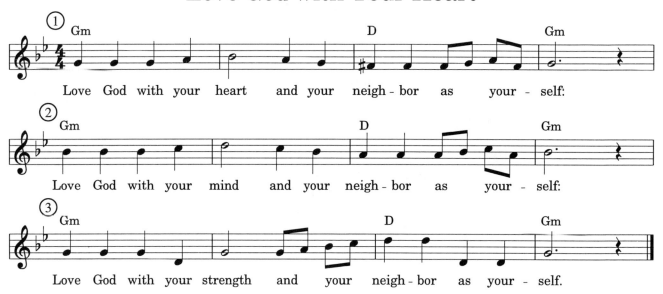

① Love God with your heart and your neigh-bor as your-self:

② Love God with your mind and your neigh-bor as your-self:

③ Love God with your strength and your neigh-bor as your-self.

* May be sung as a 3-part round.

WORDS: adapt. from Mark 12:30,31
MUSIC: Traditional folk melody

Sing this haunting melody in a three-part round. Make sure one or more strong leaders are assigned to each part. If the children are not able to sing parts, consider using instruments such as a flute, recorder, or solo organ stop to play the other parts of the canon. Consider using this folk round as a companion song to "The Great Commandments" (page 112).

DISCIPLESHIP

Reach Out in Love

1. Reach out in love, reach out in love.
2. Reach out in faith, reach out in faith.
3. Reach out in hope, reach out in hope.

WORDS and MUSIC: Sharon Dale

This happy tune uses a syncopated rhythm (accent off the strongest pulse) that gives it a bouncy character. The syncopation occurs with each "reach out" except the last one. Practice this rhythm by saying the words and clapping or playing rhythm instruments with the syncopated words. After the melody is learned, try a reaching out gesture at those places.

(Ruth Anfinson Bures, reprinted from Summer 1990 *Quarter Notes,* p. 6)

I Have Decided to Follow Jesus

WORDS and MUSIC: Traditional

Arr. © 1990 Graded Press

God Gave to Me a Life to Live

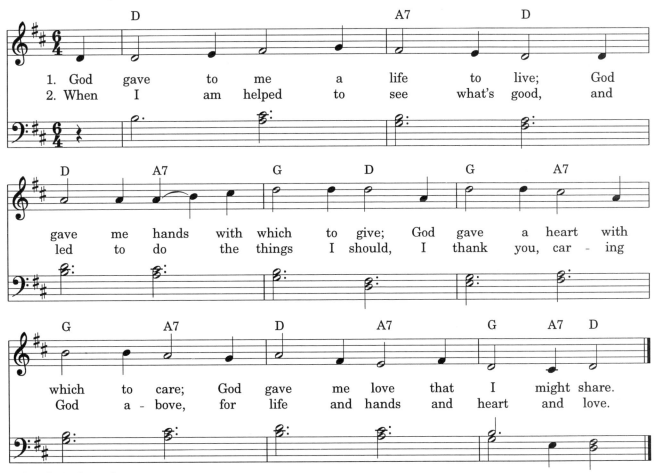

WORDS: Traditional
MUSIC: "Puer Nobis," melody from *Trier Manuscript;* adapt. by Michael Praetorius

There's a Spirit in the Air

WORDS: Brian Wren
MUSIC: Medieval French melody; harm. by Richard Redhead

Ask the children who the "Spirit" is and what the Spirit's message is. Discuss how the love of Christ is "revealed, living, working, in our world," and ways we can "tell the world what God has done."

Gladly Give

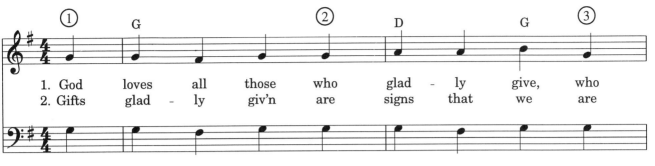

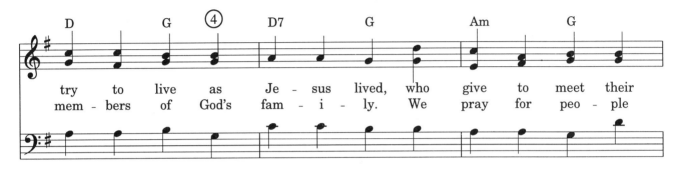

May be sung as an a cappella *4-part round.*

WORDS: Pat Floyd
MUSIC: "Tallis' Canon," Thomas Tallis
Arr. © 1970 Graded Press; words © 1990 Graded Press

Thomas Tallis, who wrote this tune, was born in 1520. As a boy, he served as a chorister at St. Paul's Cathedral in London.

Make a picture chart to learn the words. Have the children sing this as the opening to worship, followed by an organ prelude of different arrangements of this canon to help the children become familiar with the melody. Try singing it in canon form with your congregation.

(Janeal Krehbiel, reprinted from Winter 1990–91 *Quarter Notes*, p. 7)

Children, Go Where I Send You

Stanzas are cumulative; each time a new stanza is sung, the previous stanzas are repeated from the asterisk.

WORDS and MUSIC: African American spiritual

Arr. © 1988 Graded Press

Make picture/number flash cards that represent the text. Let different children be "the keeper of the cards," showing the right card at the appropriate point in the song.

Jesu, Jesu

Refrain

Je - su, Je - su, fill us with your love, show
us how to serve the neigh-bors we have from you.

1. Kneels at the feet of his friends, si - lent - ly wash - es their feet, Mas - ter who acts as a slave to them.
2. Neigh-bors are rich and poor, neigh-bors are black and white, neigh-bors are near and far a - way.
3. These are the ones we should serve, these are the ones we should love; all these are neigh-bors to us and you.
4. Lov - ing puts us on our knees, serv - ing as though we are slaves, this is the way we should live with you.
5. Kneel at the feet of our friends, si - lent - ly wash - ing their feet, this is the way we should live with you.

WORDS: Tom Colvin (based on John 13:1-17)
MUSIC: Ghana folk song; arr. by Tom Colvin; harm. by Charles H. Webb
© 1969, 1989 Hope Publishing Co.

Ask the children how they can serve their neighbors. Discuss the significance of Jesus washing his disciples' feet. Since the melody of the song comes from Ghana, teach the children something about this country and the people who live there.

Ain't Goin' Study War No More

Goin' to lay down my sword and shield down by the riv - er - side, down by the riv - er - side, down by the riv - er - side. Goin' to lay down my sword and shield down by the riv - er - side. Ain't goin' stud - y war no more. Ain't goin' stud - y war no more, ain't goin' stud - y war no more, ain't goin' stud - y war no more, ain't goin' stud - y war no more.

Chords are for the key of A.

WORDS and MUSIC: African American spiritual

Discuss the text of the song with the children. Mention peacemakers of the past and present, and the attempts of nations and individuals to attain peace in the world. Ask the children how they can be peacemakers.

Hiney Mah Tov

* May be sung as a 2-part round.

WORDS: Psalm 133:1
MUSIC: Israeli Round
Arr. © 1980 Graded Press

Dayënu

First time - Leader
Second time - All

I - lu ho - tsi, ho - tsi - a - nu, ho - tsi - a - nu mi - Mits - ra - yim,
(ē - lū hō - tsē, hō - tsē - ā - nū, hō - tsē - ā - nū mē - mēts - rǎ - yēm,

ho - tsi - a - nu mi - Mits - ra - yim, da - yë - nu.
(dǎ - yā - nū.)

Refrain (all)

Da - da - yë - nu, da - da - yë - nu, da - da - yë - nu, da -

1. yë - nu, da - yë - nu,

2. yë - nu, da - yë - nu.

WORDS: Based on the *Haggadah*
MUSIC: Hebrew folk song

Arr. © 1991 Graded Press

This Jewish folk song is often sung as part of the Passover celebration. It celebrates the good things God gave the Jewish people through the covenant, and their deliverance from slavery in Egypt. The literal translation of this song is "Had God done nothing more than take us out of Egypt, for that alone we should have been grateful." Teach the children how to dance the hora. They may hold hands in a circle or place their hands on the shoulders of the persons on both sides of them. Movement begins to the right.

Dancing the Hora

1. Step right with right foot
2. Place left foot behind right foot
3. Step right with right foot
4. Hop on right foot
5. Step left with left foot
6. Hop on left foot

May the Warm Winds of Heaven

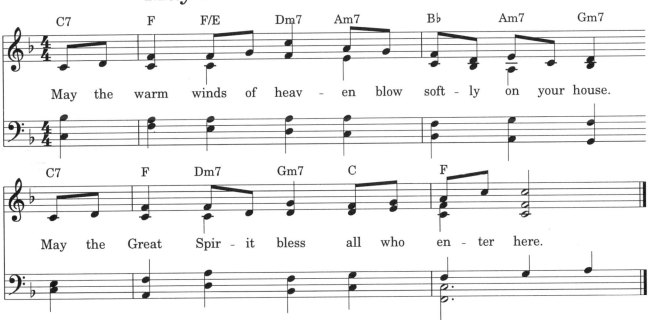

May the warm winds of heav - en blow soft - ly on your house.

May the Great Spir - it bless all who en - ter here.

WORDS: Traditional Cherokee Nation prayer
MUSIC: John Thornburg

Music © 1992 Abingdon Press

Since the text is a traditional Cherokee prayer, teach the children something about the Cherokee people and their culture.

Shalom
(Farewell, Dear Friends)

Sha - lom cha - ve - rim, sha - lom cha - ve - rim. Sha -
Fare - well, dear friends, stay safe, dear friends, have

lom, sha - lom. Le - hit - ra - ot, le -
peace, have peace. We'll see you a - gain, we'll

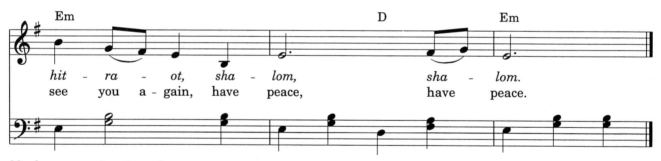

hit - ra - ot, sha - lom, sha - lom.
see you a - gain, have peace, have peace.

May be sung as a 3-part round.
Pronounced: Shah-lohm Kah-vey-reem, Leh-heet-rah-oht

WORDS: Trad. Hebrew blessing; trans. by Roger N. Deschner
MUSIC: Israeli melody, arr. Nylea L. Butler-Moore

Trans. © 1982 The United Methodist Publishing House; arr. © 1993 Abingdon Press

Go Now in Peace

May be sung as a 3-part round.

Ostinato for Keyboard, Handbells, and / or Orff Instruments

WORDS and MUSIC: Natalie Sleeth (based on Luke 2:29)
© 1976 Hinshaw Music, Inc.

Consider using this song as a closing theme song. Try the instrumental ostinati if instruments are available.

Da Pacem Domine
(Grant Us Peace, O Lord)

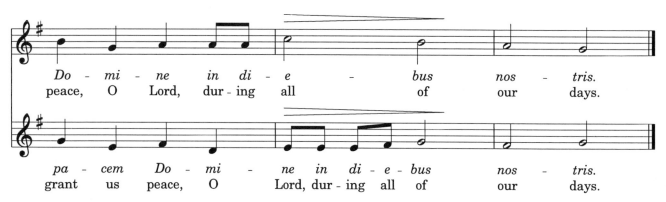

WORDS and MUSIC: César Franck

This simple two-part song can be used during devotional time or as a closing song. Learn about the noted romantic composer, César Franck, and share this with the children.

We, Your Children, Praise You

WORDS: Lois Horton Young
MUSIC: Franz Joseph Haydn

Words © 1981 Graded Press; arr. © 1967 Graded Press

Lead the children in a study of the composer, Franz Joseph Haydn.

Sing for Joy!

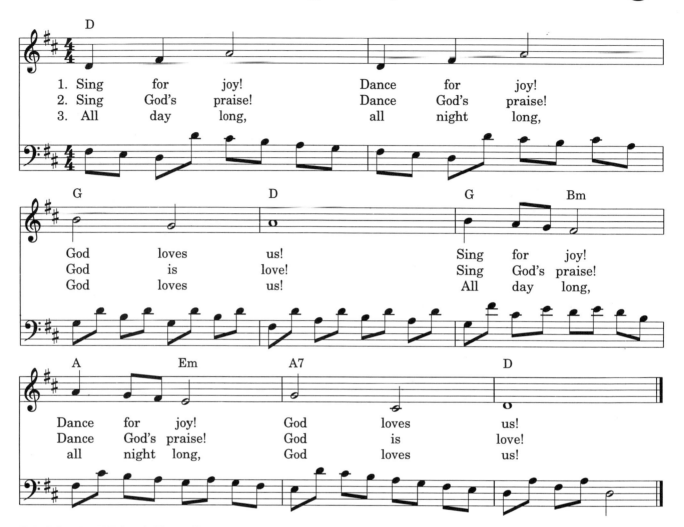

WORDS and MUSIC: Lois Horton Young

Choreography by Rosalie Branigan

Introduction: Children enter on the introduction and form one or more circles, depending on space and number of children. The taller children form the back of the circle and the shorter ones the front (Figure 1).

Stanza 1: "Sing for joy! Dance for joy!" Facing in and holding hands in the circle, skip to the right, or counterclockwise (Figure 2).
   "God loves us!" Stop skipping and still holding hands, lift arms high and look up to heaven. Older children can bend backward slightly and lift their heads up and back.
Repeat the movement moving left, or clockwise (Figure 3).

Stanza 2: All children turn and face the congregation. Each child skips around in a tiny individual circle, in place, doing the following arm movement. (Younger children can omit the skipping and only do the arms.)
   "Sing God's praise" Extend left arm, shoulder high, palm up and sweep the right hand, palm down, back and forth over it in the deaf sign for singing. End with two quick claps on the word "praise," the sign for praise (Figure 4).

"Dance God's praise" Starting chest high, roll both hands around each other, while raising the arms overhead. This is the traditional ballet mime for dance. Again end with two quick claps, this time with the arms overhead, on "praise" (Figure 5).

"God is love" Leave arms overhead, reaching up, and continue skipping till the word "love." At this point, stop facing front and cross both arms across the chest, hands in fists, in the sign for love. Repeat the movement on the next three lines (Figure 6).

Stanza 3: All face into the circle or circles again.

"All day long" All run into the center of the circle, arms reaching up over head (Figure 7).

"All night long" All turn and run back, facing out, with head laying in the crook of a bent right arm as if sleeping (Figure 8).

"God loves us" Reach arms up over head on "God." Bring arms in across chest in sign for love and kneel on one knee on "loves us." Repeat movement on the next three lines (Figure 9).

Come, Christians, Join to Sing

WORDS: Christian Henry Bateman
MUSIC: "Spanish Hymn," arr. by Benjamin Carr
Arr. © 1967 Graded Press

Find this hymn in your hymnal, and let the children sing it from there. Children need to know the great hymns of the church so they can join with the worshiping community. Use this hymn during "together time." Even the youngest children could join in on the "Alleluia! Amen!" sections. Add instruments on "Alleluia! Amen!" Praise to God should sound joyful!

(Reprinted from *VBS 1987 Music and Activities Manual,* p. 18)

Praise God
(¡Alabadle, Oh Niñitos Todos!)

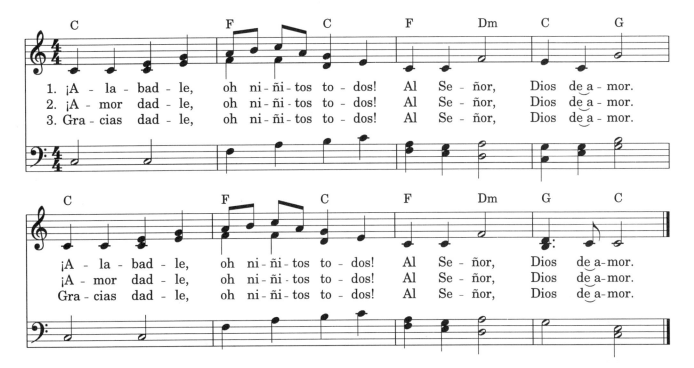

English words:

1. Praise God*, praise God, all you little children,
   God is love, God is love.
   Praise God, praise God, all you little children,
   God is love, God is love.

2. Love God*, love God, all you little children,
   God is love, God is love.
   Love God, love God, all you little children,
   God is love, God is love.

3. Thank God*, thank God, all you little children,
   God is love, God is love.
   Thank God, thank God, all you little children,
   God is love, God is love.

Optional Texts:
1. Praise him, praise him
2. Love him, love him
3. Thank him, thank him

WORDS and MUSIC: Traditional
Arr. © 1985 Graded Press

Ask the children how God shows love. Use pantomime to represent words: "Praise"—lift hands up; "All ye little children"—point to children in class; "God is love"—cross arms on chest; "Love"—cross arms on chest; "Thank"—fold hands in prayer. Make a banner of hands that praise, love, and thank God. Have the children put their hands in tempera paint and then on a piece of fabric, or have them trace their hands on paper or felt, cut out, and glue to burlap or posterboard.

(Reprinted from *VBS 1987 Music and Activities Manual,* p. 7)

Praise the Lord

1. Praise the Lord, praise the Lord, for the green - ness
2. Thanks to God, thanks to God, for the gift of
3. Glo - ry to God, glo - ry to God, for the grace of

of the trees, for the beau - ty of the flow'rs,
friends in Christ, for the church, our house of faith,
Christ, the Son, for the love of par - ent God,

for the blue - ness of the sky, for the great - ness of the sea;
for the gift of won - drous love, for the gift of end - less grace;
for the com - fort and the strength of the Spir - it, Ho - ly God;

praise the Lord, praise the Lord, now and for - ev - er.
thanks to God, thanks to God, now and for - ev - er.
glo - ry to God, glo - ry to God, now and for - ev - er.

WORDS: Nobuaki Hanaoka
MUSIC: Japanese koto melody, "Sakura"; arr. by Nylea L. Butler-Moore, based on actual Koto performance of "Sakura"

Ask the children what things they are thankful for. Since the melody of the song comes from Japan, teach the children something about the country and the people who live there. You could also introduce the children to the koto, a stringed instrument for which the "Sakura" melody was originally written.

PRAYER, PRAISE, AND THANKSGIVING
WORLD COMMUNITY

Alabaré
(I Will Praise My Lord)

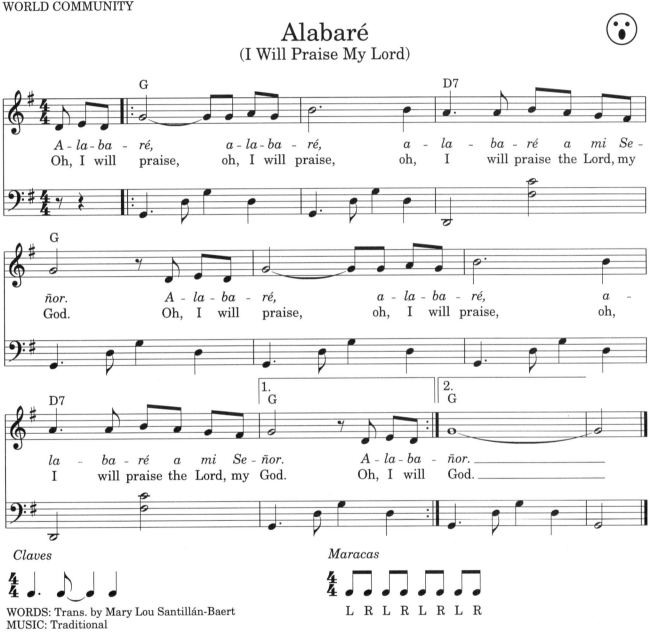

Claves

Maracas

L R L R L R L R

WORDS: Trans. by Mary Lou Santillán-Baert
MUSIC: Traditional

Trans. © 1991 Graded Press; arr. © 1982 Graded Press

The pronunciation for this Hispanic song of praise will be easy for the children to learn: ah-lah-bah-RAY ah me say-NYOR. Children love to echo. Have half of your group sing the first two and last two "alabarés" while the other half echoes immediately. You may occasionally wish to substitute the words, "Oh, I will praise" for "Alabaré," finishing with "Oh, I will praise the Lord my God."

(Joyce Whitehead Elliott, reprinted from Spring 1991, *Quarter Notes*, p. 7)

Praises to the Lord

WORDS: Lois Horton Young
MUSIC: Melody from the Spanish Renaissance; arr. Gary Alan Smith
Words © 1982 Graded Press; arr. © 1993 Gamut Music Productions

Let the children count the asymmetrical measures out loud: "1-2-3-4-5-6-7, 1-2-3-4-5, 1 and 2 and" in order to get the feel of the song. (Notice that the eighth note is constant.) Then, sing the notes while counting. When the children can successfully sing and count, try adding the words.

PRAYER, PRAISE, AND THANKSGIVING

Blessed Be the Name

WORDS and MUSIC: USA campmeeting chorus (based on Psalm 72:19); arr. by Ralph E. Hudson

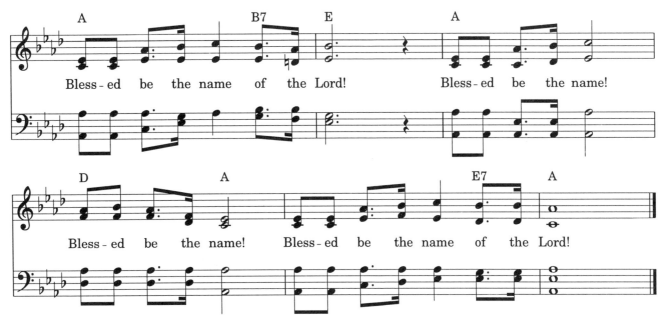

Bless-ed be the name of the Lord! Bless-ed be the name!

Bless-ed be the name! Bless-ed be the name of the Lord!

* Chords are for the key of A.

Come, Let Us Gather

Come, let us gath - er now and sing prais - es and thanks to

God our King. God's love is great - er than an - y - thing.

* May be sung as a 3-part round.

WORDS and MUSIC: Traditional

Arr. © 1987 Graded Press

Consider using this three-part round as a "gathering" or opening "theme" song. If the children are not able to sing the song in canon, use one or two instruments to play the other parts.

Jesus, We Want to Meet

1. Je - sus, we want to meet on this thy ho - ly day;
2. We kneel in awe and fear, on this thy ho - ly day;
3. Thy bless - ing, Lord, we seek, on this thy ho - ly day;
4. Our minds we ded - i - cate on this thy ho - ly day;

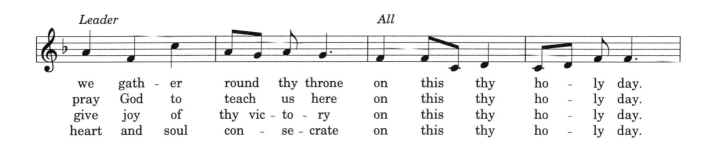

we gath - er round thy throne on this thy ho - ly day.
pray God to teach us here on this thy ho - ly day.
give joy of thy vic - to - ry on this thy ho - ly day.
heart and soul con - se - crate on this thy ho - ly day.

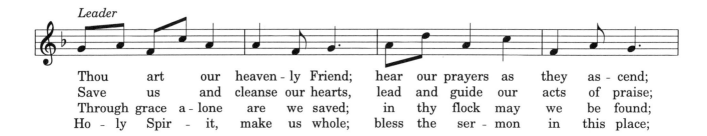

Thou art our heaven - ly Friend; hear our prayers as they as - cend;
Save us and cleanse our hearts, lead and guide our acts of praise;
Through grace a - lone are we saved; in thy flock may we be found;
Ho - ly Spir - it, make us whole; bless the ser - mon in this place;

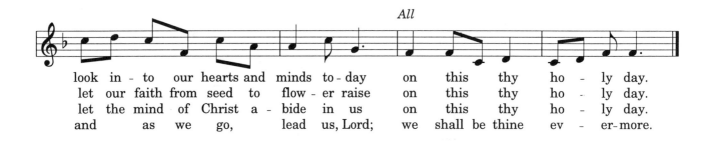

look in - to our hearts and minds to - day on this thy ho - ly day.
let our faith from seed to flow - er raise on this thy ho - ly day.
let the mind of Christ a - bide in us on this thy ho - ly day.
and as we go, lead us, Lord; we shall be thine ev - er - more.

Optional Drumbeat Patterns

WORDS: A. T. Olajida Olude; trans. by Biodun Adebesin; versed by Austin C. Lovelace
MUSIC: A. T. Olajida Olude

This song is an excellent Introit or Call to Worship. The "All" sections can be quickly learned, and the "Leader" part can be sung by a child, youth, or adult soloist.

Send Me, Lord

WORDS and MUSIC: Trad. South African (based on Isaiah 6:8)

Since this song comes from South Africa, teach the children something about the country and the people who live there. Discuss what it means to respond to God's call.

Jesu Tawa Pano
(Jesus, We Are Here)

Brightly

Je - su ta - wa pa - no; Je - su ta - wa pa - no;
Je - sus, we are here; Je - sus, we are here;

(except last time) Mam-bo Je - su.

Je - su ta - wa pa - no; ta - wa pa - no, mu zi - ta re - nyu.
Je - sus, we are here; we are here for you.

WORDS and MUSIC: Patrick Matsikenyiri
© 1990 Patrick Matsikenyiri; trans. © 1990 Iona Community

Bring out the drums and make up your own part! Here is an original composition by Patrick Matsikenyiri, a leading figure in contemporary African church music. It is a joyful call to worship, "Jesus, we are here for you." Here is an opportunity to find Africa on the globe and to remember that the Christian family is around the globe. The African church is growing rapidly, and vibrant music is important to worship there. (Dan Stokes, reprinted from Winter 1991–92 *Quarter Notes*, p. 7)

PRAYER, PRAISE, AND THANKSGIVING

Alleluia

1. Al - le - lu - ia, al - le - lu - ia, al - le - lu - ia, al - le - lu - ia,

al - le - lu - ia, al - le - lu - ia, al - le - lu - ia, al - le - lu - ia.

WORDS and MUSIC: Jerry Sinclair

2. He's my Savior
3. I will praise him

© 1972, 1978 Manna Music, Inc.

Make sure the children know that "Alleluia" is an expression of praise and thanksgiving. Let them make up their own verses.

Do Lord

1. Do, Lord, oh, do, Lord, oh, do re-mem-ber me. Do, Lord, oh, do, Lord, oh, do re-mem-ber me. Do, Lord, oh, do, Lord, oh, do re-mem-ber me, way be-yond the blue.

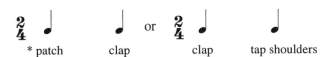

2. I took Je - sus as my Sav ior, you take him too. *etc.*

WORDS and MUSIC: Traditional

Use this song when teaching the story of the repentant thief who was crucified next to Jesus (Luke 23:39-43). Let the children make up simple body ostinato patterns such as:

2/4 ♩ ♩ or **2/4** ♩ ♩
* patch   clap   clap   tap shoulders

* Patch is short for *patschen*, a German word meaning to slap legs or thighs

Wonderful Book of God's People!

Won-der-ful book of God's peo-ple! Won-der-ful book of God's Word! In the Bi-ble pa-ges, passed down through the a-ges, the voice of God is heard! Oh, won-der-ful book of God's peo-ple! Won-der-ful book of God's Word! A book full of trea-sure, let's all learn to-geth-er what

WORDS and MUSIC: Pamela Chun Wilt

© 1993 Cokesbury

94

Hi-Ho, How Do I Know?

Refrain

Hi - ho, how do I know? Be - cause the Bi - ble tells me so!

Hi - ho, how do I know? The Bi - ble tells me so!

1. It tells of God who made us and loves us one and all, for
2. It tells of men and wo - men who fol - lowed God's com - mand, and

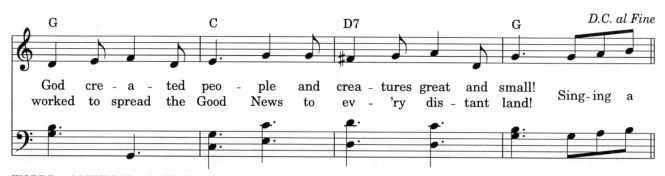

God cre - a - ted peo - ple and crea - tures great and small! Sing-ing a
worked to spread the Good News to ev - 'ry dis - tant land!

WORDS and MUSIC: Natalie Sleeth

Elijah Rock

WORDS and MUSIC: African American spiritual

Arr. © 1991 Graded Press

Once the syncopated rhythms are thoroughly learned, have the children snap or clap on the off-beats. Create simple body ostinato patterns such as:

* patch   clap

* Patch is short for *patschen*, a German word meaning to slap legs or thighs

Trust in the Lord

Come on and trust, trust in the Lord!

Trust, trust in the Lord! Ya got - ta trust,

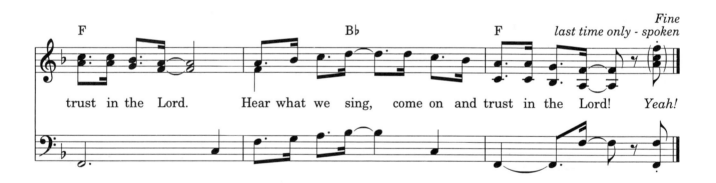

trust in the Lord. Hear what we sing, come on and trust in the Lord! *Yeah!*

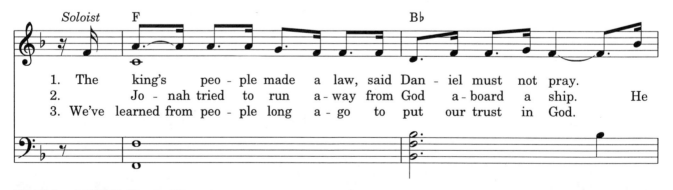

1. The king's peo - ple made a law, said Dan - iel must not pray.
2. Jo - nah tried to run a - way from God a - board a ship. He
3. We've learned from peo - ple long a - go to put our trust in God.

WORDS and MUSIC: Timothy Edmonds

Have a soloist sing the verses and let the entire group sing the refrain. You may teach one verse at a time to coincide with the teaching of a particular Bible story.

As Jacob with Travel

1. As Ja - cob with trav - el was wea - ry one day,
2. The lad - der is long, it is strong and well - made,
3. And when we ar - rive at the ha - ven of rest,

at night on a stone for a pil - low he lay;
has stood hun - dreds of years and is not yet de - cayed;
we shall hear the glad words, "Come up hith - er, you blest,

he saw in a vi - sion a lad - der so high,
man - y mil - lions have climbed it and reached Si - on's hill,
here are re - gions of light, here are man - sions of bliss."

that its foot was on earth and its top in the sky,
and thou - sands by faith are climb - ing it still:
O who would not climb such a lad - der as this:

WORDS: Anonymous (based on Genesis 28:10-22)
MUSIC: Traditional folk hymn

Refrain

Al - le - lu - ia to Je - sus who died on the tree,

and has raised up a lad - der of mer - cy for me,

and has raised up a lad - der of mer - cy for me.

Use this traditional folk hymn when teaching the story of Jacob's ladder (Genesis 28:10-17). "We Are Climbing Jacob's Ladder" is a good companion song.

God's My Shepherd

1. God's my shep-herd, ah, and I shall lack noth - ing.
2. In dark val - leys, ah, I will fear no e - vil.
3. Spreads a ta - ble, ah, keeps my cup o'er - flow - ing.

Feeds me dai - ly, ah, by still wa - ters leads me.
God is with me, ah, his staff is my com - fort.
Lov - ing kind - ness, ah, God will al - ways show me.

God re-stores my soul with love, ah, and leads me in right ways.
God re-stores my soul with love, ah, and leads me in right ways.
And I know that I will dwell, ah, in his house for - ev - er.

WORDS and MUSIC: Indian Bhajan, written down and adapt. by Leonard T. Wolcott (based on Psalm 23)
Arr. © 1989 Graded Press

Draw pictures representing the text (such as a shepherd, sheep, grass, still waters, a cup) and ask the children to improvise musical sentences based on the pictures. Then ask the children if they know any scripture that uses the images depicted.

Use a finger cymbal or light tambourine shake on "ah." Bells can play each time the "ah" occurs. Word watch: "lack," "still," "restores," "evil," "staff," "comfort," "o'erflowing," "dwell." Make sure the children understand these words.

(Ruth Anfinson Bures, reprinted from Summer 1990 *Quarter Notes*, p. 7)

Teach Me Your Ways, O Lord

WORDS: Psalm 25:4 (adpated from *Good News Bible*)
MUSIC: James Ritchie

Music © 1990 Graded Press

God Is Our Shelter

WORDS: Psalm 46:1
MUSIC: James Ritchie; arr. by Timothy Edmonds
Music © 1990 Graded Press

In Silence Waits My Soul

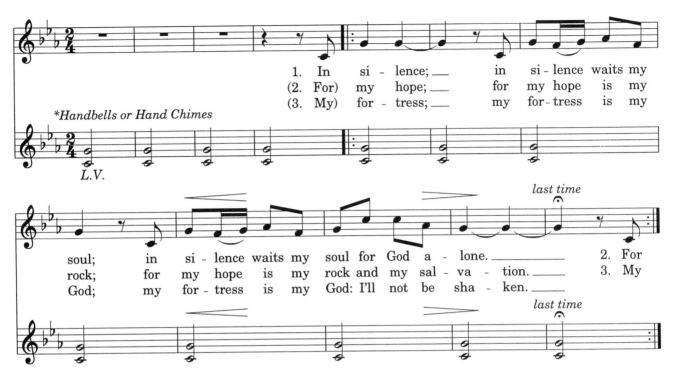

*Handbells or Hand Chimes

L.V.

last time

last time

*Play an octave lower for piano or other keyboard.

WORDS: Psalm 62:5-6; adapt. by James Ritchie
MUSIC: James Ritchie
© 1992 James Ritchie

Bible times bring to mind pictures of deserts, barrenness, struggle, and hope. The handbell open fifth lets us sense the Eastern culture. The minor melody lends itself to a feeling of longing. Read Psalm 62:5-12. Talk about God always being with us. God's presence in our hearts gives us comfort, strength, and courage. Have the children share experiences of finding comfort in God. If the concept is abstract for the age level, share a personal story. Use a prayer as a concrete example of something they will understand later: "O God, when I need a friend, help me know you are with me. Amen."

(Patty Clark, reprinted from Fall 1992 *Quarter Notes*, p. 1)

Enter God's Gates

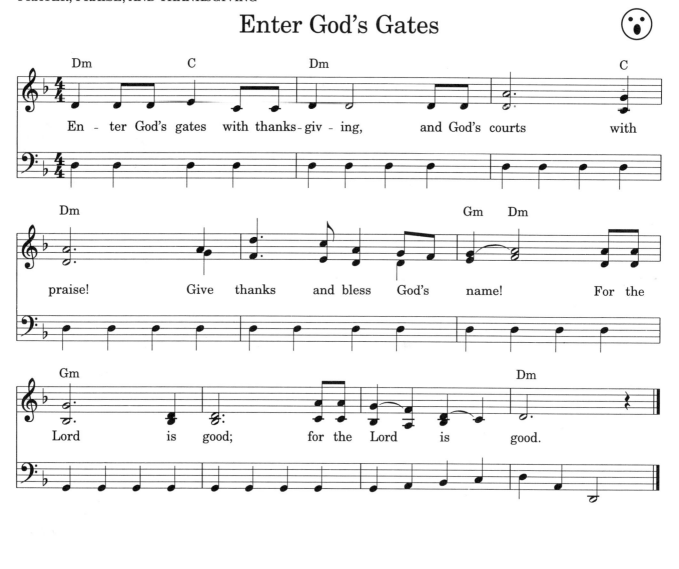

WORDS: Psalm 100:4-5a (adapted)
MUSIC: Philip R. Dietterich
Music © 1964 Graded Press

Autoharp chords are furnished with this song, and they are simple enough for children to play. If you have Orff instruments, a bass ostinato (repeated pattern) could be played on low D and A for the first six measures, low G and D for the next three, then going back to D and A for the last. Play the pentatonic melody on an alto or soprano instrument. Use a hand drum to add another dimension.

(Franklin Poole, reprinted from Summer 1991 *Quarter Notes*, p. 7)

This Is the Day

* Chords are for the key of E.

WORDS: Psalm 118:24; adapt. by Les Garrett
MUSIC: Les Garrett

© 1967, 1980 Scripture in Song

* patch clap patch clap   or   patch clap snap clap

* Patch is short for *patschen*, a German word meaning to slap legs or thighs

Jonah

1. God said to Jo - nah, "Go to Nin - e - veh,
2. Jo - nah took a ship and said, "I won't go,
4. Jo - nah preached God's mes - sage in Nin - e - veh,
6. Then God said, "Each per - son in Nin - e - veh,

Nin - e - veh, Nin - e - veh, and tell all the peo - ple of
I won't go, I won't go, I don't like the peo - ple of
Nin - e - veh, Nin - e - veh, and then all the peo - ple of
Nin - e - veh, Nin - e - veh, is a wo - man, child, or man I

Nin - e - veh, that God says you're do - ing wrong."
Nin - e - veh, so I'll be mov - ing
Nin - e - veh, said, "We'll do wrong no
dear - ly love, so why should I not for - give?"

a storm shook the ship on which Jo - nah sailed, and he
God for - gave the peo - ple of Nin - e - veh, but

spiritual; arr. by Nylea L. Butler-Moore
arr. © 1993 Abingdon Press

land - ed in the o - cean deep. But God sent Jo-nah to
Jo - nah was so an - gry he said, "Those folks were ver - y,

Nin - e - veh by means of a great big fish.
ver - y bad so why should God for - give?"

D.C. al Fine

Joshua Fit the Battle of Jericho

[A] Joshua fit the battle of Jericho, Jericho, Jericho,
Joshua fit the battle of Jericho, and the walls came tumblin' down.

[B] You may talk about your King of Gideon, you may talk about old King Saul,
but there's none like good old Joshua, at the battle of Jericho.

[B] Up to the walls of Jericho, he marched with spear in hand,
"Go blow that ram horn," Joshua cried, " 'cause the battle is in my hand."

[B] The lamb, ram, sheep horns began to blow, the trumpet began to sound.
Ole Joshua commanded the people to shout, and the walls came tumblin' down.

(Repeat A)

WORDS: African American spiritual

Both versions of this spiritual can be learned by the entire group or can be sung by a soloist in storytelling fashion.

Nehemiah's Song

Refrain

Build a wall! Make it long and tall. Build a wall! Make it safe for all! Build a wall! Don't for-get the gate. Build a wall, build a wall, build a wall!

1. I had asked some friends who came my way, how Je-ru-sa-lem had met her fate. "There is trou-ble there: gates de-stroyed by fire, and the wall is tumb-ling down."

2. When I heard those words I sat and wept, and I mourned for days. A fast I kept. And I prayed, "O Lord, be at-ten-tive to me." Then my boss said "Go and see."

3. So I fin-'lly came to see the wall, I went out at night, sur-veyed it all. Then I called my friends, set a-bout the task, and the wall was built up fast.

4. As we did the work our cour-age grew, and we fin-ished on day fif-ty two! With the help of God, all the work was done. We were changed, were God's! We won!

WORDS: Based on Nehemiah 1:2-6; 15
MUSIC: Roberta Exline
© 1987 Graded Press

The message of this song makes it an ideal one for wood block or hand drum accompaniment. Try playing on the first three beats of each measure in the refrain. This song is made for dramatizing, so choose a Nehemiah and co-builders and go to it!
(Joyce Whitehead Elliott, reprinted from Spring 1991 *Quarter Notes*, p. 7)

Seek Ye First

WORDS: Karen Lafferty (based on Matthew 6:33; 7:7)
MUSIC: Karen Lafferty

The Great Commandments

Optional Sung Responses to Stanzas 1 and 2

WORDS: Pauline Palmer Meek (based on Matthew 22:37,39)
MUSIC: Pauline Palmer Meek; arr. by H. Myron Braun

Rejoice in the Lord

* May be sung as a 2-part round.

WORDS: Philippians 4:4-9
MUSIC: Traditional melody

Sing this song in a two-part round. If the children are not able to sing both parts simultaneously, either have a soloist sing or an instrumentalist play the second part.

The Good Samaritan

1. A certain travel-er on his way was robbed and left to die. Help-less by the road he lay, and no one heard his cry. A cer-tain priest came down that way, a man most dig-ni-fied. "I will not get in-volved," said he, and passed on the oth-er side.

2. A cer-tain Le-vite came that way, a man of wealth and pride. "I'm much too bu-sy to stop," said he, and passed on the oth-er side. But a cer-tain man from Sa-ma-ri-a, a strang-er in the land, took pit-y on the in-jured man and lent a help-ing hand.

WORDS: Mary Lu Walker (based on Luke 10:29-37)
MUSIC: Mary Lu Walker; arr. by H. Myron Braun
© 1975 Paulist Press

Refrain

Don't pass your neigh-bor by, my friend, don't pass your neigh-bor by.

Love your neigh-bor as your-self, don't pass your neigh-bor by.

Read the biblical version of the story of the good Samaritan (Luke 10:29-37). After the song is learned, dramatize the story by using mime or by creating a frieze. The boys and girls could write their own script of the biblical version, or their own modern-day interpretation of the story.

Just Ask Paul

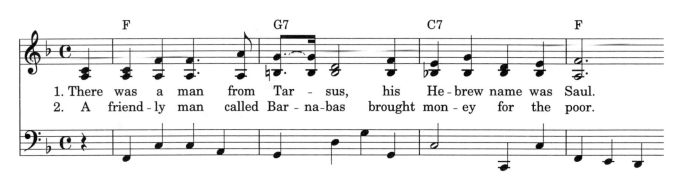

1. There was a man from Tar - sus, his He - brew name was Saul.
2. A friend - ly man called Bar - na - bas brought mon - ey for the poor.

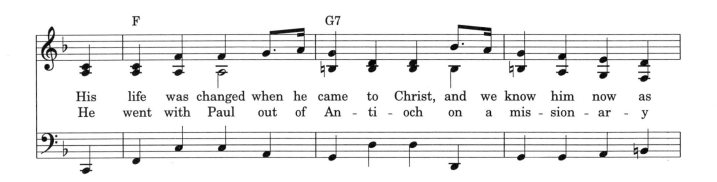

His life was changed when he came to Christ, and we know him now as
He went with Paul out of An - ti - och on a mis - sion - ar - y

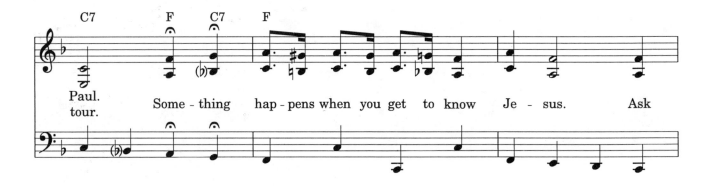

Paul.
tour.   Some - thing hap - pens when you get to know Je - sus. Ask

{Paul,
Bar - na - bas} it hap - pened to him.   When you're walk - ing down the road and you

WORDS and MUSIC: Donald F. Marsh
© 1986 Graded Press

see the light, that God is love, and love makes right, then you

want to pass it on to the whole wide world. Ask { Paul, / Bar - na - bas, } it hap - pened to

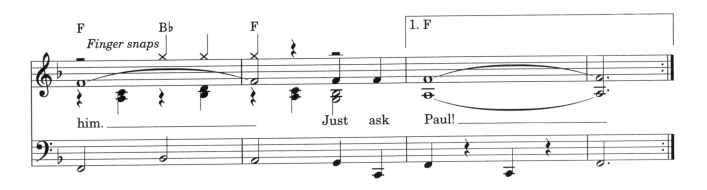

him. _____ Just ask Paul! _____

Bar - na - bas. _____ Just ask Paul! _____

What a Fantastic Creation We Are

1. This is the nose that sits here on my face; two eyes and ears help to
2. Arms used for hug - ging and hands used to touch; feet that like stomp - ing through
3. She bod - ies, he bod - ies; each one u - nique; ev - 'ry con - ceiv - a - ble
4. Some folks have bod - ies that don't work so well, still they have sto - ries they

fill up the space; two cheeks, one chin, and a mouth that can say,
pud - dles so much; God made a bod - y for you and for me.
size and phy - sique; yours is the spe - cial one God had in mind.
can't wait to tell; if we just lis - ten we'll un - der - stand how

"How thank - ful I am God made me this way."
Let us take care of God's gift faith - ful - ly.
Look in the mir - ror and there you will find:
we all fit in - to God's spe - cial plan now.

Refrain

Oh, what a won - der - ful, mar - vel - ous, glor - i - ous, what a fan - tas - tic cre -

a - tion we are! When I look all a - round I am re - mind - ed we're

WORDS and MUSIC: James Ritchie
© 1984, 1987 James Ritchie

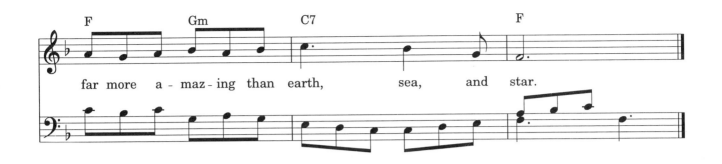

far more a - maz - ing than earth, sea, and star.

Just the Way I Am

I like me just the way I am! You like me just the way I am! God likes me just the way I am! Sing, glo - ry hal - le - lu - jah! Sing, glo - ry hal - le - lu - jah! Sing, glo - ry hal - le - lu - jah! Sing, glo - ry hal - le - lu - jah! A - men.

Variation: In place of "Amen," you might sing "I like me."

WORDS and MUSIC: Pamela L. Hughes

© 1973 Graded Press

I Am Special!

WORDS and MUSIC: Pamela Chun Wilt

© 1993 Abingdon Press

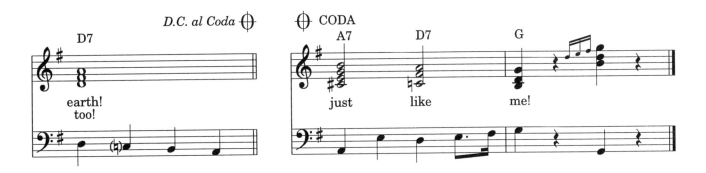

Alternate Refrain Lyrics

2. You are special,
   oh, so special,
   God made it so true!
   I can look and look and look and look,
   but I'll never find anyone just like you!
   No, I'll never find anyone just like you!

3. I am special!
   You are special!
   Isn't it marvelous?
   We can look and look and look and look,
   but we'll never find anyone just like us!
   No, we'll never find anyone just like us!

Use this song as an opportunity to talk with the children about each one's unique or special qualities. Have them share one thing they do very well. Make sure each child identifies one special quality, activity, talent, and so forth. Look around the room. We are all so different in the way we look: color of skin, hair, and eyes, and sizes and shapes of bodies. We are special people!

(John Yarrington, reprinted from Spring 1992 *Quarter Notes,* p. 2)

In Our Family

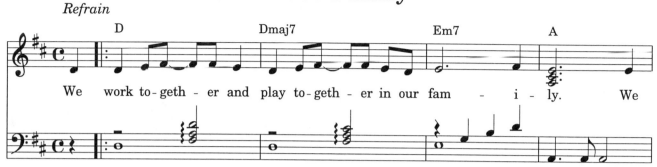

Refrain

We work to-geth-er and play to-geth-er in our fam—i-ly. We

last time - poco rit.

love to-geth-er and pray to-geth-er in our fam—i-ly.

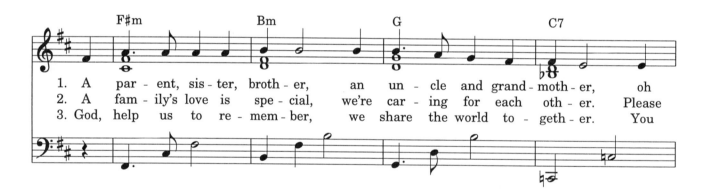

1. A par-ent, sis-ter, broth-er, an un-cle and grand-moth-er, oh
2. A fam-ily's love is spe-cial, we're car-ing for each oth-er. Please
3. God, help us to re-mem-ber, we share the world to-geth-er. You

thank you, God for mak-ing us with love for one an-oth-er. We
help us, God, to try to do our best for one an-oth-er. We
made us all, we hear your call to al-ways love our neigh-bor. We

WORDS and MUSIC: Pamela Chun Wilt

© 1993 Abingdon Press

The Family of God

Refrain

We be-long to the fam-'ly of God, a fam-'ly of those who care.

Fine

Friends who help, pro-tect and guide, the love of God is there.

1. Moth-ers, fa-thers, aunts and un-cles, broth-ers, sis-ters, too;
2. In each church, the peo-ple prom-ise to lead us in God's way,
3. Thank you, God, for ev-'ry one who lends a help-ing hand,

D.C. al Fine

heart and hand, they're part of the plan to bring God's love to you.
teach-ing us to do what's right in all our work and play.
mak-ing one big fam-i-ly, from man-y diff-'rent lands.

WORDS and MUSIC: John Horman

Love, Love, Love

1. Love, love, love! That's what it's all a - bout! 'Cause
2. Joy, joy, joy!
3. Me, me, me!
4. You, you, you!

God loves us, we love each oth - er, moth - er, fa - ther, sis - ter, broth - er.

Ev - ery - bod - y sing and shout 'cause that's what it's all a - bout! It's a - bout

love, love, love! It's a - bout love, love, love!
joy, joy, joy! It's a - bout joy, joy, joy!
me, me, me! It's a - bout me, me, me!
you! you! you! It's a - bout you! you! you!

WORDS: Herbert Brokering
MUSIC: Lois Brokering
© 1970 Augsburg Publishing House

Optional Stanza
Peace, peace, peace! That's what it's all about!

Ask the children four times, "What is this song about?" Have the children sing the answer, "It's about love, love, love" (joy, me, you). Ask again, "What is this song about?" Have the children answer by singing the song from the beginning.

(John Yarrington, reprinted from Spring 1992 *Quarter Notes*, p. 3)

Love Your Neighbor

WORDS and MUSIC: Susan Eltringham (based on Matthew 22:39)

© 1993 Abingdon Press

A Friend Is a Wonderful Thing

WORDS and MUSIC: Terry Kirkland, from the musical, *Through the Roof!*
© 1991 Abingdon Press

Activity on page 128.

127

Use this song when teaching the story of Jesus and the paralytic (Luke 5:17-20, 24b-25). Have the children draw or paint a picture of the story, or if the Bible story is not being taught, let them draw or paint a picture of their best friend. Consider the possibility of learning the entire twenty-minute musical, *Through the Roof!*. This musical could be presented with young children assisting a group of elementary-age children.

FAMILY AND FRIENDS
BIBLE VERSES AND STORIES

Two Friends

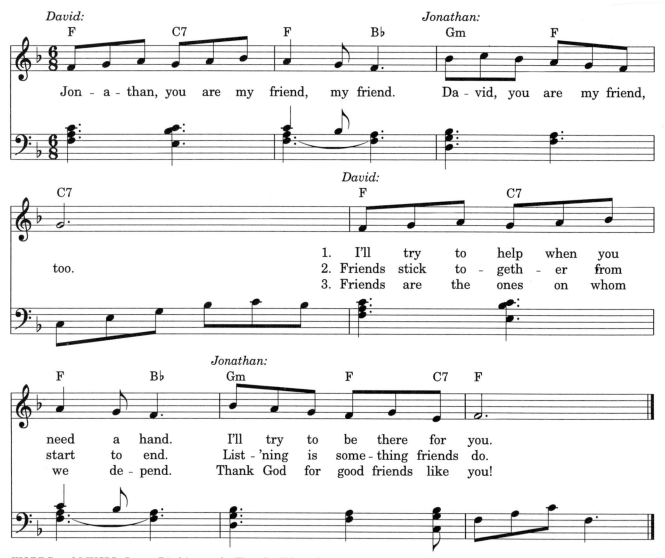

WORDS and MUSIC: James Ritchie; arr. by Timothy Edmonds
© 1990 Graded Press

Ask the children about their friends. Talk about what it means to be a friend. Divide the class into friendship pairs and have the children sing the song to each other, using their own names. Or, divide the children into two groups and have one group be David and the other group be Jonathan.
(Ruth Anfinson Bures, reprinted from Summer 1990 *Quarter Notes*, p. 7)

Index of Composers, Arrangers, Authors, Translators, and Sources

Index of First Lines and Common Titles